"Whatever happens,
happens!"

Bob B

Bermuda Suicide Challenge

in a flats boat

by

Robert Brown

AuthorHouse™
1663 Liberty Drive, Suite 200
Bloomington, IN 47403
www.authorhouse.com
Phone: 1-800-839-8640

First published by AuthorHouse 11/27/2007

ISBN: 978-1-4343-4975-0 (sc)

Library of Congress Control Number: 2007908839

Printed in the United States of America
Bloomington, Indiana

This book is printed on acid-free paper.

Dedication

I am dedication this book to my loving wife, Jill. While I was gone, without prior notice other than the camping trip, was able to handle everything while she still maintains a full time job and sells May Kay Cosmetics on the side. We're the type of parents that are involved in everything, that alone could be a full time job.

Also to all the adventurers out there that believe that there are still real adventures to be had.

Appreciation

Thanks to all the people behind the scenes that made this trip possible for Ralph. I am really glad that Ralph talked me into going with him. This was a trip that I will never forget for the rest of my life and besides I really had a great time. It's not often that two brothers who don't live real close with all the things that are going on in their individual lives, get to do something as special as this. This trip has brought us closer than we've been since early childhood and I have to say thank you for that.

Table of Contents

What is the Bermuda Challenge?

It was started by a boating magazine that offered a trophy for the quickest time. The challenge was to take a motor boat from the east coat of the United States across the Atlantic Ocean to Bermuda. On the voyage, the boat had to carry all its fuel and supplies. The vessels were to receive no help from any other boats along the way.

Troy Shields and Larry Graf broke the record that stood since 1904 by more than a day. They had to wait weeks for a good window in the weather. On September 20, 1996 they traveled from Virginia Beach to Bermuda a distance of 728 miles in a 26 foot Catamaran (sides over four feet) with twin 90 horse power four stroke outboard engines. They traveled at speeds between 21 and 25 mph taking with them 420 gallons of fuel. They averaged about 2.5 miles per gallon. They used an auto pilot and upon arrival, they had the boat shipped back and flew home.

The current world record for traveling to Bermuda by boat was set by Neil Burnie and Bill Ratllieff. They did it in 22 and ½ hours in a 30 foot Renaissance Prowler 306 catamaran (sides over four feet) powered by twin 225 horse power four stroke outboard engines. They ran at speeds up to 43 miles per hour, carrying 544 gallons of gas. They also had the use of an auto pilot.

Ralph and Bob Brown have the record for the longest nonstop oceanic voyage in a **flats boat** going from Atlantic Beach, North Carolina to Bermuda (674 miles) on May 2nd, 2007. The trip lasted 51 hours and they used 230 gallons of gas. This particular flats boat is from the Dreamboat's line called the Intruder. Its 21 foot long (less than two foot sides) and did not have an auto pilot. They broke their own record on the return trip to New York Harbor (772 miles) on May 11th, 2007. The duration was 53 hours and they used 300 gallons of gas.

Why should going to Bermuda in a flats boat be dubbed...

"The Suicide Challenge?"

The challenge would take a participant hundreds of miles away from the United States or any other land where all kinds of accidents could occur on a motorboat. Getting lost, running out of fuel, having a fuel leak and possible explosion; running into floating debris or whales and damaging the engine or hull; getting caught in bad weather and possible capsizing; motor break down, running out of supplies; equipment failure; crew member getting sick or hurt; and the list goes on and on.

The area from North Carolina to Bermuda is sometimes considered the Graveyard of the Atlantic. At least 2000 ships have gone under since 1526 when record keeping begun. The frigid water of Norway's Labrador Current collides with the warm waters of the Gulf Stream creating an assortment of boating conditions, many not so favorable. Bermuda is also the northern corner of the Bermuda triangle that extends down to Miami and Porto Rico where a lot of unexplained boating disappearances have happened.

The Coast Guard Air Station out of Savannah launched 277 rescue missions in 2007 and 290 in 2006. I couldn't find the number of missions from North Carolina's Coast Guard Air Station Elizabeth or the other types of rescue services like Cherry Pt, but I'm sure they're quite high.

April 19th, three people were rescued off a 35 foot catamaran because of a five foot gash in a hull caused by 40 foot seas and gale force winds 290 miles east of North Carolina. Their rescue chopper was sent to rescue them because their emergency beacon was triggered on. The rescue chopper after recovering the sailors had to fly to Bermuda because of strong west winds and its fuel situation. (eleven days before we left the dock in N.C.)

(the following events occurred during our departure from N.C and arrival at N.Y.)

May 7th was believed to be the largest rescue in which the 5th district Coast Guard was involved in. Their search along with others totaled more than 282,000 square miles of the Atlantic and lasted six days. The Coast Guard were attempting to rescue people 13 people from four sailboats. (Search ended the same day we arrived back in Florida May 13th).

The weather experts started taking a more concerned watch of the systems starting Thursday, May 3rd (The date we were scheduled to return to New York).

The 37 foot "Seeker", was anchored 12 miles out and their anchor wasn't holding. They were heading for certain disasters in the shallowing waters with the 25 to 40 waves with 50 knot winds. Three were air lifted by the Coast Guard chopper.

"Lou Pantai", a sailboat sailing with three men, triggered its EPIRB(Emergency Position Indicating Rescue Beacon) around 4:30 in the morning capsized and then was rerighted before it started to sink 225 miles out from the United States. They were in 50 foot seas with 70 knot winds when they had to abandon their sinking boat for a small life raft. At 7:30, a rescue plane located the refugees after they fired their flares. The plane had to circle for about two hours until the rescue chopper arrived to pluck them out of the North Atlantic. All were suffering from hypothermia and one had broken ribs.

The "Illusion", an aluminum 67 foot cutter/sloop with a crew of three was only 40 miles off the coast of Cape Hatteras, North Carolina when they turned east to try to motor with the westward wind until they lost their engine. They traveled for sixteen hours until 4:00 a.m.

Monday morning when they lost their steering. Now they were in 50 foot seas with 70 to 100 knot winds. The waves broke over the bow causing the two anchors to break loose, one ripping a large gash in the hull, so they triggered the EPIRB. At 2:30 when the chopper arrived, the seas died down to 30 to 40 foot with 50 knot winds. The boat still had a small section of sail up and the boat was still traveling at about six knots. Each crew member had to jump into the water and was met by a Coast Guard swimmer who helped him get hoisted up to the chopper. Then the chopper would pick up the swimmer, chase down the boat and wait for the next crew member to abandon the "Illusion".

The "Flying Colours" a 54 foot sailing yacht with four seasoned experienced sailors was never found. Their EPIRB first went off near 7:30 a.m. and the last one went off late in the afternoon. The last know position of the "Flying Colours" was 160 miles south east of Cape Lookout, North Carolina.

During the rescues, two of the Coast Guards were injured, but will recover. One strained his back and the other has his hand pinched in the hoisting cable.

Chapter 1
The Phone Call

Being a self-employed handyman, I was on day three of tiling my wife's parent's living room. I was at the tail end of a rather difficult tile job. I had to move the furniture, take up carpet and tack strips; clean and acid etch the floor. The carpet had been serpentined against the already existing tile, so they had me install a mosaic border, serpentined to separating the different tiles. I had to cut in half the 16-inch tile border all around the edge of the room that I cemented down along with most all of the 13 inch main tiles. These I had installed in a diamond pattern. Because every cut was exposed, it was taking a long time to cut these tiles with a large wet saw.

On Wednesday night, the night before, I worked as late as I could. I stopped when I was afraid of making too much noise. The neighbors had a problem with noise, mainly my in-law's two small dogs. The puppies loved to bark.

Leaving for the night, I knew I was going to have a hectic day for Thursday. I had an appointment with my tax accountant to do my first quarter taxes at 9:30 in the morning. (So much for my early start tomorrow morning) When I arrived home Jill, my wife informed me that Ralph, my younger brother had called to invite me on a publicity trip. Ralph had a boat company called Dreamboats. He wanted to promote his third boat model, the Intruder One, a 21 foot flats boat, that he designed, by diving it to Bermuda. He said that this would set a world record. Nobody has ever taken a flats boat to Bermuda before. Jill said that she told him, "absolutely not!" I laughed, saying Ralph is crazy; many people have traveled the open ocean in small boats and pretty much wrote it off as a crackpot idea.

On Thursday morning at about 8:30, I returned Ralph's phone call. Ralph told me about the trip, and I told him he was crazy and anyway, I was really busy. I had to finish Jill's parents' house and that I was scheduled to go on a long weekend camping trip in Georgia with Vince and Chuck, two high school friends. I was leaving at 2:00 p.m. today. I knew that I wasn't going to be able to completely finish the tile job by two, but figured that if I could get the tiles cut and glued down. Then I could maybe persuade Vince and Chuck to leave a little later today, so that I would have time to grout the floor before we left. On Sunday when I was to return, I could seal the grout and push the furniture back.

Ralph explained his plan and told me that he'd been planning this trip for about a year. Yesterday Patrick, the guy who that had planned to go with Ralph, while they were out in the bay doing their last day testing on the boat, kept getting cell phone calls all day. From the parts of the conversations Ralph could hear, "Not as dangerous as you think it is!", he had a feeling that Patrick was getting some heat about the trip. At 8:00 on Wednesday night of April 25th, Patrick said that he was sorry, but that he had to back-out. Evidently Patrick's family and family friends had been giving him a lot of grief about the danger of taking a small boat way out in the ocean. Patrick asked Ralph, "is there any way we could go to the Bahamas instead?" Ralph's answer was, "How many newspapers and magazines are going to write about us going there?"

Ralph begged me, saying he was going to loose thousands of dollars if I wasn't able to go with him. He had already paid a lot of people to be in the right places to document the trip. The photographer was flying in to North Carolina to go out in a hired boat along with the mayor and another city manager of Atlantic Beach, N.C., to videotape the departure. He also had people lined up to drive up with him from Hudson, Florida to Atlantic Beach North Carolina then take his car and trailer up to New York, while we headed for Bermuda. Then wait till we arrived in New York to trailer the boat back with us to Florida. There were also hotels already paid for. He had a national blog for about 3,500 dollars to help advertise the trip. He really sounded desperate. I still said no, I had too many bills and I was really swamped. I was starting to feel bad for him, but this was his hole that he dug himself into and it wasn't my problem. He still begged and then asked me how much money I made in a week? Then he agreed to pay me that and then some; if I would go with him. He said that two brothers making this trip would be even better for the promotion of this trip. I finally agreed after he explained the injection foam in the hulls, proving to me that the boat is unsinkable. As soon as I hung up, I got a knot in my stomach, how was I going to get this tile job done by two?

I know what Ralph was going through; I invented something once, the NTsurfstrap. It changed the attachment point of the surfboard leash to the back of the surfboard. This way the surfboard would pivot around, allowing the water to go around the board. The board would pull through the back of the wave instead of the wave pushing the surfboard thus dragging the surfer. Needless to say, I spent 100's of hours trying to make a web page; I couldn't get anyone to help me. Even when I'd give people the Ntsurfstrap for free, they'd still never put it on their board. Even with the testimonies from all the people that actually had them on their board, stating that it works great, it was still hard to convince people to try it. I talked, talked until I was almost crazy, and still no one would help. I definitely knew a little of what Ralph was going through.

At 9:15 I drove to my accountant and spent about an hour there, they also wanted me to make an estimate on removing wallpaper, texturing the walls, and painting, their kitchen in a month or so when they remodeled their kitchen. I was really in a hurry, but I didn't want to rush out without answering all their questions. Now I was really rushing to get to the in-laws.

Arriving there, I started cutting as fast as I could. I saw my mother in law as she was leaving, I still thought that I could get the tile cut and glued down before two, so I decided not to worry her and just keep working. As the clock started catching up to me, I realized that I still had no way of getting hold of Vince and Chuck, they were at work and I didn't have their telephone numbers. I still wanted to drive home around 1:30 to talk to Jill when she came home for lunch. Maybe, I'd be able to get Chuck's work number off of caller ID. I figured Jill would be just a little upset, but that she trusted me, besides this was a paying job and we needed the money. It also occurred to me that I might not be back in time for Bryan's high school award ceremony, sometime next week. Maybe I'll be able to motive Ralph to get this trip done in a hurry. I was running out of time. It was about 1:45 when I finished cutting all the tiles and I still had tools all over the place.

Jill called me on my cell when she saw my van still at her parents' house when she drove by on her way back to work. She didn't want me to be late, when Chuck and Vince showed up. I was one of those people who were always trying to do too much; thus I was usually late.

I told Jill about the trip and she didn't seem too pleased, she said that she had already told Ralph that I was not going to be able to go. That I was going to be miss Bryan's only senior high school award ceremony and that I didn't care about anyone but myself. I tried to tell her about Ralph's situation, but she didn't want to hear about it. She said that our family was more important than Ralph's crazy plan to set some stupid world record and that nobody would care about it. She was really starting to get worked up and said that I better not be late for my other son's Middle School State Championship Track Meet on Saturday, May 5th. Jonathan missed his regional qualifying race in Melbourne, because of a state cup soccer tournament, and I spent a lot of time getting permission for him to enter the Jacksonville regional race to get qualified for the state championship race. In Jacksonville, Jonathan won both his events the 1500-meter and the 3000- meter race by a large margin. She said that this state championship was my doing, and that if I wasn't here, she wasn't going to take him. Boy was she mad!

There was no way; I'd be late for Jonathan's race. I'd be hiking in Georgia till Saturday, where Ralph and crew would pick me up. We'd drive to North Carolina and leave Sunday morning for Bermuda, a hundred miles or so and we'd spend the night. Get up in the morning and drive from Bermuda to New York the next day. We'd spend Monday night in New York and drive back by car the next two days. I should be home sometime on Wednesday night, maybe in time for Bryan's ceremony. No problem.

After putting most of my tools away, some spread over the tile area out of the in-laws way. I had furniture spread all over their house, but it wasn't really in their way. They didn't need to use the dinning room and they could easily see the TV from their favorite chairs. The path through the house was at least two foot wide, sure they would be a little inconvenience, but I figured it was no worse than anybody doing a remodel and having to wait for a reorder of some item that wasn't right. Besides, they were almost never home. I'd call them in a couple of hours and explain that I didn't get a chance to get all the tile glued down, but at least everything was cut and laying in the right spots. If it was really a problem, I knew several handymen that owed me favors and at least one of them have worked with me at their house in the past. They should be satisfied with that. And if they could wait, I'd be home sometime late next week.

Chapter 2
Camping in Georgia

(Thursday, April 26th)

I arrived at home at 2:10 and Vince and Chuck were already waiting in my driveway, wondering if I had changed my mind and decided not to go. I didn't have the heart to try to talk them into going a little later, now that they were already here. I told them that I was going to only go up with them and not come back; Ralph was going to pick me up somewhere in Georgia. I was going to go with him on an ocean trip in one of his 21 foot flats boats. I really couldn't even remember the name of the island. I kept saying Bimini, Bahamas, or something like that. Even after they said Bermuda, and I agreed that that was the right one, I still kept getting the name confused. It really didn't matter; I was just going for a boat ride, no big deal. Vince suggested that I think of Bermuda shorts to help me keep the name straight.

I asked them if they knew how far Bermuda was from the U.S.? They both thought it was probably between two and three hundred miles southeast of North Carolina. I said, "that was about a hundred miles further than I thought." They both expressed some reservations, and made suggestions about what to do in different situations. First and foremost, make sure you are always tied on the boat; you never know when a rouge wave might sweep you off the boat.

As we were driving up to Amicalola Falls, Georgia. I was really feeling guilty about the unfinished tile job, so I called my in-laws. No one was home, so I left a short message on their answering machine. I figured I'd call them back in a couple of hours to explain. Still feeling guilty, I called them back later. Jill's dad answered and he let me know that he was really disappointed in me for helping Ralph and missing Bryan's award ceremony. He accused me of caring more about Ralph's project than my family. I told him, that of all the dads I knew, I had way more videos of my kids that I'd taken while at their events than anyone else.

I thought to myself, besides I even watch the tapes over and over with my kids, not like parents that take video, who would rather watch golf than any of their kids sporting events or home movies. I was really getting mad, how could anyone accuse me of not caring about my kids? I really got along well with my kids. Even as teenage kids, they still talked to me in front of their friends and most of their friends seemed to like me. I even wrestled with some of them. We'd wait for each other to watch certain TV shows together; Survivor, Lost, Prison Break, Smallville, That Seventy Show, Malcolm in the Middle, the matches of the Ultimate Fighter, and several others. We could talk about anything, and often did. Besides, Jill would video the ceremony, if I wasn't there, so I really wouldn't miss anything.

We talked about their tile job. I told him, "that if they'd like, I'd have some friends of mine finish the last couple of hours of the job."

He said, "They hired me, and not my friends. They would rather wait for me to finish the job." He wanted to know exactly when I was going to be back? All I could say was that sometime late next week.

I was really wishing that I had blown off the camping trip in order to finish the job. Vince and Chuck had asked me to hike with them a month or so ago on a different trip and I said I couldn't because of work. This trip had been planned for several weeks. These are guys, that right out of high school we were really tight, and had done several trips to the Smoky Mountains in North Carolina and to the Grand Cannon. I haven't done anything except talk with these guys in years. I really wanted to go hiking. Really good friends are hard to find and really important to keep.

We camped at Amicalola Falls and on our second day hike; we hiked the eight miles up the Approach Trail that led to the top of Springer Mountain, the start of the Appalachian Trail (AT trail). One of my two boys is dying to someday hike the whole 2172 miles from Georgia to Main. The volunteer caretaker at the start showed us where the register notebook was so I could sign it. The message I wrote for the thru hikers doing the AT, "My son Jonathan is going to do this trail someday, so please keep it beautiful by not leaving your trash. Good luck everyone!" We used the camera timer to take a couple of pictures of us with the AT plaque, before heading back down to our camp.

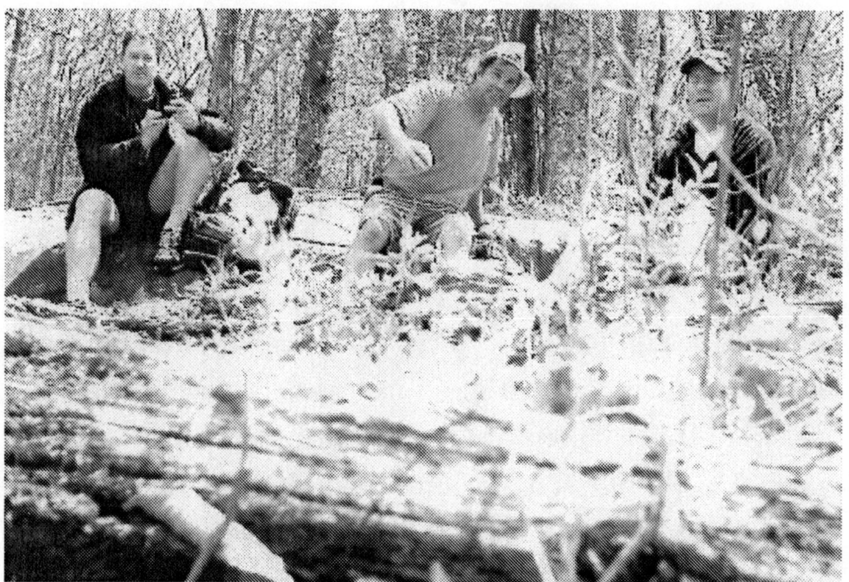

On Springer Mountain, the start of the AT trail. Posing for a self portrait before lunch. Chuck, Bob and Vince

I could hardly sleep both nights of the camping trip, because I couldn't stop thinking about Jill being mad at me, and the tile job. I'm sure Vince and Chuck were getting tired of hearing me talk about it. I was still trying to justify my trips. I called Ralph several times, asking him questions about the Bermuda trip and trying to figure out a place to meet Saturday night. We agreed to meet at a RCI, a camping store near Duluth, Georgia off Interstate 85. Chuck and Vince wanted to stop to buy some items that they needed for their climb to the top of Mt Ranier in Washington State early in July.

While waiting for Ralph, I walked down a hallway at the RCI looking for the bathroom and located a map of the United States. I checked where Bermuda was located. Holy Smokes! This is way more than a couple of hundred miles from North Carolina. I ran and found Vince and showed him the map. We estimated it to be more than 600 miles. The distance from the Florida Keys to Atlanta, Georgia!

Chuck asked again for clarification, "This boat is only 21 foot long? You've never actually seen it, much less ridden in it? How big is the motor and only one? You at least have a kicker (trolling motor) for an emergency back up? How big is your life raft? What about a wet suit or a survivor suit? What are you using for navigational equipment?"

I think he said 21 foot flats boat. I saw a picture of it on his website a couple of months ago. I don't know anything about the motors. Ralph didn't bring a life raft, the boat is unsinkable. I'm not sure of a wet suit or survivor suit, he told me to bring a good rain suit. He's bringing a Global Positioning System (GPS), a compass and a Satellite Phone.

I called Ralph; do you know how far Bermuda is from the United States? He said sure, it a little over 600 miles and about 100 miles further to New York. I asked him about his gas situation, and he said we were taking about 300 gallons. He gave me some figures for the amount of fuel he estimated that we would use. I wanted to know more about all of this. We talked for a while, where he explained some of his boat test in Florida. I was really interested with the ones where he filled the gas tanks filled with water, which actually weights more than gas. Ralph estimated his fuel consumption to be about 2.5 miles per gallon, which would gradually get better as we lightened the boat by burning off more of the fuel. His figures seemed believable.

After hanging up, I told Vince and Chuck, that I believed as soon as we hit the Gulf Stream and found some big waves, we'd turn back, I was almost ready to put money on it. We all sort of laughed about it. I kept thinking Ralph was crazy.

When Ralph showed up a couple of hours later with Jim and Cheri, the drivers helping to drive up to North Carolina and then take the trailer to New York. Chuck and Vince looked at the boat and sort of looked at each other and said, "You're taking this to Bermuda?" Ralph gave them the short version of the quality of the boat. We call the boat the Intruder 1, because it was the first 21 foot Intruder that we sold as a finished boat.

Ralph had to borrow it back from of his customers Pete and Debbie Rostel. "This isn't your boat? Why would anyone lend you a boat of this size to travel over 1300 miles across the open Atlantic without an escort boat?"

"I'm going to trade them a new boat with a couple of other options, after the business get going. This trip is to help promote my company, Dreamboats Inc. and hopefully contract some investors." replied Ralph.

The Intruder has a seven foot eight inch beam, the width of the boat. The canary yellow bottom is made of up to twelve layers of fiberglass and has twin 23" wide tapered hulls at their widest point that are molded in one unit called a monocat hull. The whole hull is injected with foam, making it incredibly strong and unsinkable.

The six foot front deck has a total of six hatches with double latches that make them water-resistant and four fishing rod holders built through the deck. On the floor just behind the front deck were two large coolers, for dry storage.

In the center of the boat was a large yellow console containing two cabinets, one above the other. The windshield was bronze smoked tinted flat across the front with returns on both sides. Attached to the front was a two-person bench seat with a back rest cushion. Above was the T-top shade kit made of stainless steel and white canvas. On the bottom side of the canvas top there were two large zipper storage compartments, one in front and one in back, used mainly for storage of the life preservers. Between them was a large white fiberglass cabinet with a smoked tinted door. On the top of the back of the T-top were four fishing rod holders. Two were for flags, the U.S. and the Dreamboat's logo. The raised captain's seat was a two-person bench seat with a backrest all attached to a two inch stainless steel framework.

On each side of the console were two 50 gallon white plastic see through tanks and an aluminum 70 gallon in front of the console. The standard 18 gallon black plastic tank was under the console. On top of the back deck, to the front was a white ten inch bench seat that was also the hatch cover for longer items. On each side of the back deck was one small hatch to the front and one fishing rod holder on each back corner. This Intruder was powered by a gloss black Suzuki 115 four stroke and a black six horse power kicker.

Jim and Cheri shook my hand and said that they were glad that I was going with Ralph on this trip. They said that it was a great boat and not to worry about anything. I wondered if they had ever been for a ride, but kept it to myself.

I would have loved to of heard Chuck and Vince's discussions as they drove away about the boat and the trip across the 600 miles of open ocean. Chuck had sailed, on a big sailboat, a couple of times with some of his friends to the Bahamas only about 70 miles off the coast of Florida. He said that the Caribbean is no where near as dangerous as the unpredictable North Atlantic.

Chuck, Vince, Bob and Ralph up in Georgia where I got my first look at the Intruder One

Chapter 3
Heading to North Carolina

After a couple of hours, I realized we weren't going to make it to Atlantic Beach, N.C. tonight. I was ready to drive straight through the night, but we stopped at a hotel in South Carolina. Shoot! Now I was going to be even later getting home. Maybe, we'd be able to leave as soon as we arrived in North Carolina?

(Sunday, April 29th)

By the time we arrived at Atlantic Beach, and did all the shopping for food and supplies, the day was almost gone. We had gone into numerous stores, looking for a parachute flare. We finally found one, but could not locate a Bermuda chart. It seemed that everyone had them programmed into their GPS. I was trying to decide how bad I would need a warmer jacket, since the jacket I brought on the camping trip, accidentally went home with my sleeping bag and pillow in Vince's van. After seeing the pricey price tags on all the jackets that would keep you warm it they got a little wet. I decided the sweaters and sweatshirts would be enough, with my rainsuit on the outside. It was kind of fun in the grocery store; we were like kids in a candy store. We wanted plenty of food on board in the event that we were stranded out at sea.

Ralph handed out some of his dreamboat flyers to anyone that would take one.

Ralph and his friend Paul, who was the video-photographer for the departure, were busy trying to finish wiring the remote video cameras on the Intruder. They had to buy another VCR after 11:00 at night. I was busy making a windscreen to use to try to block some of the wind and water that might blow into the boat from the side. I wished I had a sewing machine to stitch rope along the perimeter. The best idea I could come up with was to use the same glue, E-6000 that I used in my NTsurfstrap kits to glue the straps to surfboards. I folded the cloth over the 3/8" rope and held it down for a couple of seconds with a bead of glue. When it was completed, I slid it under the boat, so the dew wouldn't mess it up. It really should have at least 12 hours to dry under dry conditions, the label on the glue says three days, but the cloth is breathable and I've found that it will work on surfboards in a little as two hours, because the strap was breathable.

I tried to duck-tape up the four fishing rod holders, because they would let water get into the two of the up front storage compartments. The water would still drain out, but we didn't want any extra weight up front. Since everything was damp from the dew, the tape wouldn't stick, even after wiping it down with a towel first. I'd try again tomorrow.

We could have easily spent another couple of days rigging the boat up for a trip like this. I would have really wanted to rig the camera up so that we could see the whole boat and us at one time, maybe on a long pole that hung off the back of the boat or maybe a kite of some kind……...

I went up to bed and turned on the TV to wind down. I was watching the Most Dangerous Jobs, 'The Deadliest Catch', when I got a few butterflies and started to wonder what I had gotten myself into. The boat was unsinkable, so as long as it didn't blow up with all the fuel and the motor didn't quit, I had nothing to worry about, so I didn't. My favorite saying for the trip was "what ever happens, happens!" we'd just deal with it then. I worried no more.

Newspaper Article

From: Hernando Today in Florida

By Tony Holt (published April 29th, 07)

Success or suicide mission?

Hudson—Flats boats are made for shallow water fishing.

Ralph Brown designed his boat thinking it could withstand a cross—oceanic trip.

Then people laughed at him.

Anyone familiar with Brown's history knows how he interprets such a reaction. It is the same as daring an Olympian to break a world record.

Today, Brown is leaving the coast of Atlantic Beach, N.C. with his brother, Bob, in his 21-foot flats boat. And they are aiming to break a record of their own.

They are taking the Intruder 21 south to Bermuda and are expected to arrive by noon tomorrow. From there, the brothers will travel northbound and are scheduled to finish their unprecedented journey Friday morning at Liberty State Park in the New York Harbor.

"We're trusting this boat and nothing else," Brown said. "Except God."

Brown will be bringing three global positioning system devices, one radio beacon device and one satellite phone—not to mention a stash of coffee.

He was carrying a tall cup of joe last Wednesday, the morning before he and his friend took the boat out on the water for one of its final trail runs. He confessed he was reliant on the drink.

"I haven't figured out how to do it yet, but I'm going to," Brown said of his attempt to have coffee available throughout the trip.

Another requirement for the 1,400-mile, seven-day journey is fuel—lots and lots of fuel.

In spite of the small size of the boat, it will include four 50-gallon tanks, one 70-gallon aluminum tank and about 18-gallons internally. When Brown and his brother leave Atlantic Beach this morning, they will have 288 gallons of fuel on the boat.

On Wednesday, he filled the tanks with water, which weighs more than gasoline. He and his friend tested whether the boat would ride with so much weight. They took it out a few miles off the coast of Hudson Beach and back without a hitch.

"This is how it's going to be," Brown said as he filled the tanks using a water pump.

The ride itself was bumpy. The boat sunk lower than normal, so when it reaches speeds of up to 15 mph, a lot of the seawater splashed into it. Nonetheless, Brown expects to make great time. He was still able to accelerate up to 23 mph while all of the tanks were mostly full. In all, the boat was carrying 2,400 pound of water.

The boaters expect to get, on average, about four miles per gallon during the trip.

Brown, who lives in Spring Hill, owns and manages Dream Boats Inc. He designs the boats and he and a group of subcontractors build them. His business is located in Hudson.

Five years ago Ralph started the company by purchasing a business license online for the price of $232. The couple had little money and were raising three children.

Ralph a devoutly religious man, is still happily married and the father of two boys, ages 15 and 14, and an 11-year-old daughter. Anne is traveling to Bermuda this week to meet her husband and brother-in-law. The men will refuel and perhaps share a meal before Brown kisses his wife and embarks on an even longer journey to Jersey City, N.J. the site of the Statue of Liberty.

He calls his trip the Ultimate Bermuda Suicide Challenge.

During his trial run Wednesday, Brown laughed when his wife called. He gave the phone to a reporter accompanying him on his boat ride so he could hear how Anne feels about the trip.

"I think he's nuts," she said. "That's him though. He's always pushing the envelope. I just hope and pray he gets there."

Brown has already begun blogging the trip on his company's Web site (www.dreamboats.net). He and his brother drove to Atlantic Beach Saturday.

Brown is taking a video camera to film what he thinks is the longest-ever unescorted cross-oceanic ride in a flats boat. Similar stunts may have been done, but not without an escort, he said.

He will contact Guinness World Records when he and his brother return. Brown wants the world to know what his boats are capable of.

"No one will laugh when we're finished with this trip," he said.

(Monday, April 30th)

Ralph woke up early; I felt like I had finally just fallen asleep, it was time to start getting ready. We loading up the boat with all our stuff from the hotel and emptying out the back of his car. We were running out of space on the boat fast. The large coolers in the front were stuffed with everything that we wanted to be sure would not get wet. In the end, we stuffed things anywhere we could find a place. We had to fuel the boat up with about 300 gallons according to Ralph. Paul met us up at the gas station, where the commotion started, people were finding out about our trip mainly from Ralph talking to anyone who would listen. He also had all the window of his car painted with signs like Bermuda or Bust! Most of them commented about the size of the boat, if we'd be able to carry enough gas, and that they wouldn't try it in anything less than a 30-foot boat. Most made sly remarks barely loud enough for us to hear to their friends. I spent over an hour fueling up the boat, they never make the vents big enough, the gas always wants to burp up and get you. I tried to speed up the fueling by holding the nozzle up high enough for the air to escape out around the fill tube. It was only a couple of times that the nozzle slipped above the fill tube and sprayed gas on the deck of Ralph's Intruder.

We had to be cleared for the credit card by the cashier several times during the process. The total bill was almost over 900 dollars. After doing the math, four 50-gallon tanks, one 70-gallon tank, and the original 18-gallon tank under the counsel; 288 total gallons. Paul was busy videotaping a little of everything, from almost every conceivable angle. After remembering what Chuck said while camping, I decided to be safe and grabbed an extra two gallons of water, Ralph started to question it, but quickly decided it wasn't a bad idea.

Arriving back at the Palms Hotel, we drove around to the back preparing to launch the boat. I checked the drain plugs on the twin hulls while Ralph went over to be introduced to the Mayor and City Manager from Atlantic Beach. I followed him to the pavilion where Mike, the captain of the chase boat, was sitting waiting for us. With Paul filming, Ralph and I shook everyone's hand. It was time to launch the boat. Mike offered to drop it into the water, since it was a small, narrow ramp. But Ralph said he would do it, and drove the trailer into the water before we switched places. I drove the trailer the last couple of feet to get the boat to float off, while Ralph started the motor and backed the boat off the trailer. The wheels of the trailer were submerged over the wheel bearings before the boat came off the trailer, due to the 2000 pounds of fuel; the boat was quite a bit heavier than usually. The boat floated extremely low in the water, but as the fuel is used up, the boat will rise in the water. Ralph had purchased a grease gun so that Jim could regrease the wheel bearings before towing it to New York. It's always a good idea to force the salt water out of the wheel bearing before going a long distance with a trailer.

Remembering how many times I've been seasick on diving and fishing trips, I located my bottle of 12 Dramamine pills. I had a tough time finding them in the grocery store yesterday since I didn't know what kind of packaging they came in. I finally gave up and asked the girl working the register. Even with her directions, I spent over ten more minutes looking before retracing my steps to the original section I first started looking; they were hanging on a hook, not on the shelf. Anyway, I decided to take one a few minutes before we were to shove off.

Mike had the Mayor, after signing some paperwork witnessing our departure, climbed into his blue twin-engine custom-made boat, which Mike actually made. The city manager had a busy schedule that day and wouldn't be able to escort us to the edge of the bay. With Paul filming from the escort boat, we pulled out from the Palm's Hotel dock at 9:15, Monday April 30th, leaving from Atlantic Beach at Beaufort Inlet southeast of Morehead City, N.C.. We brought the Intruder one, the first Intruder 21 to ever be sold, up to a little more than idle speed, then up to cruising speed. We were so involved in arranging the boat and heading out, that we almost clipped a large buoy in the middle of the channel. We missed it by inches, we looked at each other and I wondered if Paul had recorded that on video. We almost ending the trip before it even started, but in reality, nothing would have happened, we'd just bounce off. Worse case scenario would be a small crack in the rail, or damaging the buoy, which we would have had to report, possibly delaying the trip.

Since the bay was so calm, I used this time to duck-tape the fishing rod holders that I wasn't able to do last night. Then sat back and video taped a little of everything. I was having a good time and a little excited. I was a little worried I'd get sea sick and have a terrible time. (Who wants to go 600 miles up chucking all the way?)

We continued on until we reached a blockade. The Navy was in the process of turning an enormous military ship around, and all the boaters had to wait till it was turned to a certain spot before they would give us permission to pass. Mike yelled out to the commander, that we were in a hurry; we have a boat heading to Bermuda. The commander looked at the Intruder and said it will be a few more minutes. Then, instructed us to back away from the Navy Carrier. He probably just noticed the multitude of fuel tanks.

While waiting, we kind of went over a last minute check of our provisions: American Flag, dreamboat flag, Sat phone, lighted compass, 2 fire extinguishers, EPIRB, Hand held Radio, mounted GPS, hand held GPS (eats batteries), lots of batteries, 2 orange life jackets with flashing white light and whistle, 2 regular life jackets, digital fuel flow reader, Suzuki 115 engine, 6 horse power kicker, 288 gallons of gasoline, 2 tool boxes, box of assorted wire connections, 6 gal jug of water for reserve, 2 and a half gals for use, hand held video camera, 2 remote wireless video cameras, with 2 VCRs in cabinet, about 20 blank VCR tapes, 3 boat batteries, several flare guns with flares, parachute flares, 1 store bought sea anchor and one home made, regular anchor and lots of rope, personal clothes, rain-suit (Walmart quality),motorcycle rain suit, my cell phone, old digital camera, go-pro surf wrist camera; lighter plug in mug warmer, crock pot and grill; lots of black 8 inch plastic wire ties, 2 head lamp lights, 6 volt flood light, 12 volt light that clips to battery, 2 throw cushions, four bottles of sun-screen, one bottle of

12 Dramamine tables, 2 quarts of engine oil, four pairs of sun glasses, 3 hats, couple of pens, Ralph's notepad of telephone numbers, hand pump to transfer fuel and 3 wired in bilge pumps, 2 trolling fishing rods, casting rod, small tackle box full of fishing equipment, a bunch of give away dreamboat T-shirts and a stack of dreamboat flyers to hand out.

This is when Ralph realized he didn't have his black berry cell-phone. He must have left in his car along with his mug of coffee.

Food that we brought for the trip from North Carolina to Bermuda: 8 and a half gallons of water, almost 2 gallons of blue Gatorade, four cans of fruit cocktail, 8 cans of soup, small bag of potatoes, 1 bag of carrots, 1 bag of Nachos, 1 can of cheese dip, bottle of chicken bullion cubes, spray Pam, crunchy peanut butter, squeeze bottle of strawberry jelly, bottle of Italian dressing (for fish if we catch any), loaf of bread, bag of oranges, Fig Newton cookies, jar of peanuts, Saltine crackers, box of raisins, two boxes of granola bars, box of graham crackers, Ritz crackers, 6 frozen hamburger patties, half gallon of milk and a box of cereal.

Chapter 4
Out to Sea

Once the war ship was swung far enough around, so that the aft end was away from the center of the channel we were told we could pass to the far right. Now that we were out in the bay, we could pick up speed. The escort boat was following off to the left most of the time, while Paul videotaped. They sped up and took pictures from in front, and more as we passed them. We waved a lot. They called us over to stop and the mayor explained that she had to get back to work. They drove ahead for a few minutes while we drove over their wake. Mike explained for us to go straight-ahead, past the barrier islands then ver off to the north to cut across the shoals. This would save us at least 20 minutes. We motored over to them one last time, so Ralph could throw Mike and the Mayor a dreamboat T-shirt, before waving goodbye and heading for the opening to the Atlantic.

As we were rounding the point of Cape Lookout, we were close enough to shore to see a rusty white van parked on the beach with some people fishing. We went straight out about a hundred yards, while watching the waves break on the shallows; we turned north just to the outside of the breakers. I made the comment that one of us should go to the front and watch for shallowing water. Ralph laughed, and reminded me, that if we were on plane, even with all the extra weight, we'd still be barely drawing any water. About ten minutes later, we changed our heading for Bermuda. The GPS said we were to travel on a course of 110 degrees for about 670 miles. That's the first time that I realized that Ralph had down played the distance, he said it was more like 600 miles, the reading stated that it was more like 700 miles. Oh, and the 300 gallons of gas was more like 288 gallons. But we were on our way, "What ever happens, happens!"

Leaving Atlantic Beach, North Carolina, picture taken from escort boat just before they turned around near the mouth of the bay.

We were both excited now that we were actually on our way. We both should have been dead tired, but we were wide-awake. As we scanned up and down the coast, we were about the only boat in sight. There were just a few small fishing boats close to shore and it seemed that we were the only ones heading out to open water. We supposed that we'd see a bunch of boats during our crossing, since we figured a lot of people go to the Bermuda, and North Carolina was the shortest distance to it.

Now that we were on our own, we used this time to rig the boat, with a safety line from the front cleat back to a cross bar on the T-top frame just over the front bench seat. On that, we tied another line with a loose loop to slide along the first rope. Our tether rope was so short that there was no way to fall off the boat. On the other end, we put a large carabiner that we used to clip onto our belts whenever we were on the front deck of the boat. We also tied a short rope off the framework of the captain's seat for the back deck safety line. After a while, we got tired of the hassle of using our belts, the belts were too wide, it was hard to fasten and unfasten from the carabiner, the thin edge of the belts kept getting caught in the inner locking notch of the carabiner. We both tied a rope belt around our waist and used that to attach the carabiner to.

It wasn't too long before I saw water spouts about 50 yards off the right side of the boat. Ralph didn't get a chance to see it. I kept looking hoping to see a fin or the back of what I assumed was a whale, but I never did. Still wearing long pants and a shirt, I was soaked and decided to put my motorcycle rain suit on over them. Ralph put on his Walmart rain suit. Even though we were wet, we were still comfortable now that our rain suits kept most of our body heat in and blocked a lot of the wind. We were mainly getting wet from the water the boat threw into the air and the wind blowing it back at us. The seas were still relatively small, probably two to four feet; with a big chop from the 15 to 20 miles an hour wind mainly blowing out of the South West. The swells were traveling faster than we were; they were basically traveling in the same direction and we were quartering them just a little bit. We were still riding heavy in the water midway through the day. The average mile per hour on the GPS was between 13 and 18 miles per hour with the engine running at about 4200 rpm. We had decided to try to drive the Suzuki 115 engine between 4000 and 4500 rpm, which was what Ralph and his mechanic had decided, was a safe rpm as to not strain the motor since we were running with a power prop instead of a speed prop. They decided to use the power prop because of the added weight of the fuel.

Mid afternoon we ran across a pod of dolphins. There had to be at least 20 of them not more than 40 yards out in front of us. They crossed our path without even slowing down. We were hoping that they would follow us, or come over by us. Most of them were swimming on the surface, just arching their backs to barely break the surface. I thought this is going to be great, in day one whales and dolphin. We're going to see so much wild life. I was hoping to see some sharks or manta-rays close to the size of our 21 foot boat.

Ralph brought along two large trolling fishing rods, I guess they were really deep-sea rods and a regular size casting rod. One of his dreams on this trip was to catch a large fish while trolling. I really wasn't too keen on the fishing part. I was really still in a hurry to get to Bermuda than back to New York, I wanted to be home for Jonathan's track meet, since I had already given up on Bryan's award ceremony. Normally I would have loved to have slowed the boat to about 8-mph and taken our time. I too would have loved to catch a huge sailfish or something, especially since we had video equipment. Although with no ice or anyway to save a large fish, we would have just taken pictures and let them go. The fishing equipment was really for survival in the event that we got stranded out here for several extra days. Ralph tried trolling and eventually broke his rigs, we were traveling too fast, he'd try again later.

Since, we forgot to get ice at the gas station, like we planned. Ralph ate a cup of cereal with milk; we also left the two bowls and spoons in the back of his car. Setting the milk on the still frozen hamburger patties, we figure we'd have cereal one more time before we'd have to pour the milk in the ocean. Ralph eventually had more cereal before we trashed the remainder of the milk. I ate chips and had fruit cocktail. The bread was already smashed; we planned on eating it later. The thawed burgers were also donated to the Atlantic for fish food, since now it was too rough to stop and try to cook them on our 12 volt plug in grill.

Now that we were in the deep blue waters of the Gulf Stream, the waves picked up a foot or two. But it still wasn't bad. I remember the first big wave we rode over and went down the face at a slight angle. The Intruder slid just a little side ways. I yelled "Woo ah!" just for a second and it was over. Now that was kind of fun! Now we started looking for the bigger waves. The boat was still heavy, but we could still get a little thrill from riding down the face. Every once in a while, we'd sneak in a bottom turn, pretending the boat was a surfboard.

Every now and then the fiberglass cabinet underneath the T-top, but above our heads would pop open. We were afraid of loosing some of our electronic equipment; almost all of it was stored up there. We bungeed the door shut.

Early in the afternoon, we saw a big sail boat way off in the distance behind and to the north of us. Ralph kept making his wish list; he wanted to see a cruise ship up close somewhere near the mid-way point. We were going to ask them to video tape us and send us a copy; that never happened. We saw several flying fish and some were even quartering our deck. I kept watching for one to make a mistake and land in the boat.

Sometimes during our hand held video taping, we'd jump up to the front deck and video tape a 360 degree view. Even though we agreed we'd always be clipped in, we often found ourselves up front, just holding onto the rope without a life jacket. Usually the driver would have to remind the photographer to clip in. Even though we might have been going through three to five foot seas at the time, we always felt perfectly safe. (That's usually when accidents occur.)

Since we knew we'd basically be up for the next couple of days, we would try to get some sleep anytime we could. We were able to take short cat naps laying down on either the front deck, which was usually too rough with the boat slamming down after going over a large wave or on back bench seat over the storage compartment where we usually got splashed by the rouge waves.

Ralph woke me up, when he spotted the whale off to our left and started driving over in that direction. He said he saw a waterspout then the back and tail of a whale. We drove over to the spot he reported seeing the whale and we discovered a large swirl in the water much larger than the 21 foot Intruder. He wasn't so sure he wanted to be this close. What would happen if it came up and nudged us? He decided it was time to get a move on. I'd had been on some whale watches off Cape Cod, Massachusetts and was excited at the prospect of spotting one up close. Ralph mentioned something about the possibility of it having a calf and protecting it. Needless to say, we motored away at a rapid pace.

Ralph suggested that we should try to hang up our wind block that I had made the night before. We decided to fold it in half, so that we could see over the top. It was designed to go up to the front cleat but we didn't really need in up front so we jury rigged up on the front support of the T-top, ending it even with the windshield. We were a little concerned how the winds would affect it. We installed it on the right side of the Intruder, because the wind was blowing from our right rear cleat. The wind block worked great. It was small enough not to catch too much wind and yet large enough to block most of the wind and water.

Whenever we stopped for Ralph to make phone calls, we had to idle because of the noise: The constant hammering from the boat pounding against the waves, the wind whistling by flapping everything hanging, combined with the engine, was too loud for Ralph to hear the person on the other end of the line.

Ralph idling as he talks to Paul, his web master, on his rented satellite phone. Notice the homemade wind block rapped around the frame of the T-top on left.

Soon, it was time for one of us to really try to get some sleep. Dressed in our rain gear, we took shifts sleeping on the ten-inch bench cushion just in front of the back deck. It was usually just a waste of time we'd just lay there looking out over the water watching the waves come right up to the edge of the boat and lift the boat up and slam it down. With the waves slowing getting bigger, the larger ones were approaching six foot. They looked even bigger when you were laying down almost at water level and looking up as the swells came up from behind whenever they were traveling faster than our boat. When we were going faster than the swells, we'd see large patches of white water being thrown back away from the boat as we cut through the waves and chop. Often the wind would carry the water back toward the person lying on the back.

We usually slept with our heads tucked behind our home made wind block, but the bigger waves that we were quartering (hitting at a slight angle) would actually send buckets of water over the angling down edge of our wind block and still clear our heads. That was most of the time; every once in a while; depending on the angle we hit the waves and the amount of wind. Sometimes the sleeper would get the full force of the splash and the first reaction, after the high pitch girlish scream, was to kill the driver, who was instantly apologizing. We always woke up freezing, and just shivered for about ten minutes until we warmed up.

The driest place on the boat was the captain's chair, from there the windshield and wind block made a nice shielded spot to drive behind. While standing we could see over the top of the wind block and when it was really cold, we could sit and be protected. Usually whenever the sleeper woke up, both of us would sit on the captain's chair, with the driver always on the right. Some one was always driving, because we did not have a auto-pilot, like probably almost every boat that has ever driven to Bermuda, even sailboats have auto-pilots systems.

We often snacked on food, which seemed to help warm us up. We tried to heat up some soup with the lighter plug-in mug warmer. This was the kind that looked like an Arby's curly fry that hung on the inside edge of your cup. It didn't heat up at all even though a lot of the soup was splashing out of the mug. The soup eventually went over the side. I didn't say anything, but I was ticked, I planned to be drinking steaming hot soup and bullion all night long and I'm sure Ralph had instant coffee on the brain.

Going to the bathroom wasn't too hard, thank goodness for zippers. We'd usually throttled the boat down, tilted the mounted video camera up and shortened the back safety line by wrapping it around the framework of the back seat and then fastening it to the rope around our waist. The first couple of time we went off the sides leaning over the railing behind the 50 gallon gas tank, but we were bounced around a lot and didn't have much stability since the railing was so low, it only came up a little below our knees. Ralph later discovered it was easier to go off the back, while holding onto the top of the engine to steady ourselves; we'd pee into the ocean. Going number two would be accomplished by hanging your rear end out over the edge of the boat with the safety line in front. Ralph discovered he had to be careful after getting his tail washed by a big wave.

We videotaped using the hand held tape recorder whenever we had a chance; the only problem was that everything was wet. At first we had a plastic bag wrapped around the camera and taped to the outside of the lens. With all the wind, the bag was always flapping in front of the lens. Soon I ripped the bag off. We stored the recorder up in Ralph's large cooler where he kept his dry clothes, which was a pain to get to. We decided to make it more accessible so we stashed it in the canvas zipper bin in the bottom of the T-top over our heads.

The Intruder was starting to look lived on. We had Bungees threaded through the arms of shirts fastened to the string weaved through the eyelets of the canvas shade kit on the T-top. Our sneakers were also hanging by their laces with other wet articles hung wherever possible. The only problem was they really weren't ever going to dry. Just when they were almost dry, somehow a wave would splash them. Ralph followed my lead after loosing his hat in the ocean, by tying a string to his remaining hat then to his belt.

We had been using a little fuel from each of the tanks to balance out the boat. Ralph's engineer Marino had installed a series of valves so that it was really easy to switch tanks. Most of the valves were underneath the back bench seat on both sides of the boat. The only tank not on this system was the large metal 70-gallon in front of the bench seat. We were saving it for after all the 50-gallon tanks were empty because it was in the center of the boat and to the front of the console. We wanted to keep the weight in the center and also a little to the front to help keep the boat on plane. Since the 70-gallon tank wasn't hooked into the system, we would every now and then get a wife of gas fumes in the air. It really bothered me, to be smelling fumes. Especially since I knew we would be riding like this for at least 24 more hours until we used up the other tanks and hooked into the system. Ralph didn't seem to care since it was only a whiff every now and then. We eventually modified the vent on it; by attaching the 3/8"-fuel supply line that was hanging loose for later when the other tanks were empty. We looped it and attached it to the vent line to try to prevent fuel from splashing out the vent. It worked great! We didn't smell any fuel in the air any more.

We changed the VCR tapes in the VCR earlier in the day and noticed that one of the tapes was still at the beginning. Ralph almost left it in but since we had so many, we decided to switch it out too. When it was time to switch out the tapes the second time, Ralph noticed that he couldn't see the dim red lights around the inside of the rim of the cameras. The batteries that were in the remote cameras were dead. He was under the assumption that the batteries should have lasted the whole trip. It wasn't easy, but we tried to hook up a charger, using the wires that came with the cameras. The batteries showed no signs that they were recharging. We left the wires hooked up in case it took a while.

Digging around in my storage cooler, I discovered the little black bag that my surfboard lock came in. I brought the lock with us in case we needed to lock something up. The bag was a sort of web bag and would be great for storing some of the little items that was bouncing around the dash and some of the stuff we needed to get it easily. I tied the bag to the outside upper framework of the T-top. It was loaded up with sunscreen, chapstick, several of Ralph's cheap reading glasses, extra pair of sunglasses and anything small enough to fit in it. Later it was a pain to get the glasses out in a hurry, because the arms would work their way through the bag and get caught on the hinge. But it was still better than having them bounce on the deck.

The sun was setting with a beautiful sky. There were hardly any clouds and the sky had a rainbow of colors. Almost white right at the horizon which turned to yellow, orange, pink, red and then bands of different shades of reddish purple until what was left of the darkening blue sky. I pulled out the video camera and filmed about five (thirty second) sequences about five minutes apart. On the last sequence all the bright colors were gone just leaving several shades of purple and gray. I had some shots with the camcorder sitting on the front deck and the sunset would come in and out of view as the boat was lifted up and down by the waves. I had several good shots of the Suzuki engine with the sky in the background.

When night finally came, I was pleased to see that we had a full moon. We were getting a little tired of the boat bouncing up and down and were looking forward to when we thought the seas would die down at night. The sky was incredible, even though the water never even calmed. The stars were also coming out, but not as many as I thought we'd see.

We were in luck; the moon was coming up in the east, just a little south of our heading. We were able to keep our heading of 110 degrees

S.E. by keeping the moon to the right of the first support for the T-top. Without a land or sky mark, it was hard to stay on the same heading unless you kept a close watch on either the compass or the GPS. Sometimes we'd look down at the GPS and discover that we were turned 90 degrees from the direction we were trying to maintain. Because the boat was so short, it was easy for the boat to pivot to the left on the waves caused by the waves coming from a slight angle from behind and also since the wind was always blowing between 15 and 25 mph. Also the longer a boat is the longer it takes for the boat to turn. With a short boat a small movement of the motor will make the boat swing around much faster.

It took me a while to get used to using the GPS. I mainly used the function with the arrow and the heading degrees. It was confusing to turn the boat so that the arrow and the red line on the degree circle would line up. Then Ralph suggested bringing the red line to the arrow. If the red line was to the right of the arrow, then by turning the steering wheel's top center to the left, the lines would come together, that was your heading. Boy did that make it easier. Just keep the arrow and the red line on top of each other and you were going the right direction.

The compass was a floating degree ball that pivoted in all directions. What ever the degree facing the driver was the heading the boat was going in. There was a black line in the dead center facing the driver. When the degree heading needed was to the right of the line; then by rotating the top center of the steering wheel to the left you would bring the degree toward the black line.

It was hard to keep the lines together. Almost every time I looked down, the course was off at least ten degrees. As the boat rode over a big wave and the wind and current pushed the boat just a little, the course was changed. Now that the moon was in the sky, we had something to follow. As the moon rose in the sky, it soon was too far to the right to use as a heading. Next appeared a planet that at first I thought was a plane with its lights on. It rose exactly in front of us, so we used it as a sky mark. Soon it was also too far to the right and then a star rose in the sky right in front of us. This made it easy to drive the first half of the night. Once the moon was to our back, we were still able to get a fix on our direction using its reflection. First we would ride in the side of the reflection, then the middle, then the other side. A lot of the time, if we were paying attention we could tell our direction by the directions the waves were moving. If we weren't slicing through them at a slight angle, we'd have to adjust. But using the waves was a pain, I hardly ever paid attention to them, but Ralph seemed to be quick on noticing if I was off course.

I wanted to get a look at the North Star, but because of the full moon, and the fact that I was too lazy to get out of the driver's seat and look around the T-top top, I never got a chance to see it. Vince and Chuck, during our camping trip, talked in great length about its location among the big and little dippers. It wasn't the brightest star, like I thought it was. Two stars of one of the dippers pointed to it, and all the stars in the sky rotated around it. I should have listened better, or at least got up to try to see it.

It was hard driving at night. It was so cold; we were really bundled up with anything that was warm, our only problem was that nothing was dry. We had agreed that at night, we'd wear the thick heavy life jackets with strobe light and whistle. These were really uncomfortable, unless you were trying to sleep sitting up, then it made your neck disappear and your head sort of balanced on top. We'd snack on anything, as long as we were eating; it was easier to stay awake. But eventually the driver would nod off, and the first big wave we ran into, we'd wake up. At least there were no cars to run into.

Late in the night, we saw a cargo ship way off in the distance. We've only seen two boats since we departed; I thought that was incredible, so much water and we were all alone. The sea never let up; we were still running in three to eight foot seas, with the wind up to 35 mph. The whole ocean looked like a large washing machine, everywhere we looked; all we could see was the moon's reflection off the spewing white caps that were everywhere. We joked about the miles left to go, how far from shore we were, and why we hadn't seen more ships. We thought this was a shipping lane, we figured we'd see a ship at least one every couple of hours.

(Tuesday, May 1st, second day at sea)

As the sun was just about to come out of the water; it started to cast a gold glow in the water. The higher it rose, the wider the track was. I felt like I was in the Wizard of Oz following the gold trail in the water. We were riding just to the left of the glow.

By morning, we were starting to really lighten up. Once the sun was up, I wanted to get out of my long wet jeans that I knew I should have never been wearing in the first place. Once they get wet, they stay wet, not like some of the expensive camping clothes that wick the moisture away from your skin that I was too cheep to buy before we left North Carolina. During the night, I ripped out the crotch of my motorcycle rain pants while stepping on the boot straps designed to go around the outside of riding boats, while leaning over. I took Ralph's fishing knife to them. I replaced the jeans with my bathing suit and my dreamboat T-shirt with my navy blue long sleeve Ron Jon's surf rash guard. The bottom six inches of my first time worn white shirt was stained a light brown from the tanning in my leather belt that I also shouldn't have gotten wet. My rain-suit went right back on, but at least I could start warming up.

Feeling better, I noticed we were staying pretty much around 20 mph, only the average time wasn't showing it. Ralph was always slowing us down with all his phone calls, which I understood was a necessity; he was trying to keep everyone informed of our whereabouts. I had used the phone several times too. I called Jill and left messages on the phone's answering machine. We are an extremely busy family, so we're not often at home till really late. Also, the kids don't often answer the phone, because of all the solicitors. I was using the SAT phone and I'm sure they had no idea who was calling on the caller ID.

At the halfway point, it was 1:00 pm on day two, 31 hours into the trip at mile 337. We celebrated with a hoot, and then studied the fuel situation. We had traveled half the way to Bermuda and only used up about half of the fuel. Neither of us seemed to be concerned. We remarked about the guys at the gas station saying we'd never be able to carry enough fuel. I figured the Intruder was a thousand pounds lighter and not pushing as much water; we'd be able to go faster and get better fuel economy.

Digging out all his papers to get his notepad, Ralph came across his wad of dreamboat brochures that were partially soaked. Without a second's hesitation, he whipped them over the side. I screamed, "Wait!" But it was too late. I asked him, "now what are you going to hand out?"

"They were soaked! I can't hand them out." Ralph remarked.

"We could have dried them out later. Something is better than nothing." I answered.

After a few phone calls, which was a pain for Ralph, he had all the phone numbers spread out among several pages of a large notepad a quarter of an inch thick. I thought to myself, on the return he'd need to put all the important numbers on a single piece of paper and tape it to the dashboard. Also, we'll need to find some sort of mattress or raft to improve the sleeping on the boat.

I was glad that I hadn't brought my computer laptop out with us. I had considered bringing it in its case and wrapping it up in several plastic trash bags. Thinking that some of the trip would be calm and I could have worked on my fiction surfing book that I've been working on since last summer. My kids were going to help me write it, but they haven't written a single page yet. Ralph and I talked about some of the stories and characters in the book, many from our high school days that have been modified and sometimes exaggerated. I did bring a pad and some pencils, but they were tucked away never to be brought out during the crossing. What I should have brought was a digital recorder.

Out of nowhere the motor started shuttering like it was running out of gas. That was impossible! The 50 gallon tanks were semi-transparent and the tank was almost two thirds full. Just as the motor died, Ralph had me check the water separator and it showed very little water. We'd take an old can (usually a fruit cocktail can) and drain the separator by twisting a drain screw. The water would empty into the can. It would take almost a full reservoir before it would stop the fuel going to the engine. I suggested that maybe there was some plastic from the inside of the tank blocking the suction tube. We unscrewed the locking nut and twisted the suction tube around until it popped up. After examining the clean screen in the end, we noticed that the tube was only about ten inches long and the tank was about two and a half foot tall. Somehow who ever sold this tank to Ralph had installed a short suction tube. We switched the suction tube with one of the other empty 50 gallon tanks. The Suzuki started right up and purred perfectly.

Several of the flying fish and squid landed in the boat. One small squid actually hit me in the head, although we didn't find the three inch squid till later. At the time, I assumed that some how I was hit by some of the hanging articles around the boat, although from the captains seat, that seemed impossible. The other surprising thing was the number of small birds skimming over the waves. We'd see one or two every couple of hours.

Sometimes we'd see big hunks of floating debris and almost every time we checked it out, there would be several large fish hanging out. As long as we stayed about 15 yards away, they didn't scatter. I couldn't identify the fish, but I've heard from some of my fishing friends that cobia, dolphin (the fish) and other good eating fish hang out under floating trash or seaweed. These would be good for the casting rod. The most common debris was wooden 4 by 4's; many over eight foot long, luckily we never hit one.

By now, Ralph had completely given up on his trolling for big fish. All his rigs keep breaking. We were traveling too fast. The speeds recorded on the GPS were starting to be between 18 and 22 mph, but we were still killing our average by the phone calls. We still left the throttle at about 4200 rpm, that Suzuki was running perfect.

We started to play a game as the boat was light enough to catch the waves now and we could ride them. The swells were traveling between 16 and 20 mph. When we ran up the backside of a large swell, the boat would come off plane, and we'd slow down to somewhere around 13 mph. As the boat slowly gained speed, we'd be watching over our shoulder for the large swells, the eight footers. As the swell crept up under the Intruder, it would lift the boat up in the water. As the swell reached the middle of the boat, the boat would start to pivot downward and we'd gain speed. Soon we'd be screaming down the face and riding really fast on plane. We would stay near that speed until we'd run up on another large swell and eventually come off plane. We watched the GPS and read off the high speeds. Ralph won the overall game with the speed of 28 mph. Yes, the boat could go faster, but in the game we weren't allowed to ever touch the throttle. We always kept the Suzuki running at about 4200 rpm. As the boat sped up, the rpm's would climb up to 5000 rpm, but soon would come back to the original 4200 rpm. As the boat lightened, we'd sometimes have to adjust the throttle down, to keep it in the 4200 rpm range.

Often, I would find myself daydreaming about surfing the swells, they really weren't steep enough to catch on a surfboard without being towed, but hey, we had rope, just no board or skis.

I was mesmerized watching the swells. The top layer of water looked like a blanket with thousands of small 1 to 2 foot chop with the tops resembling snow covered mountains with the winds blowing the snow off, just like in the movie Vertical Limit, when the storm hit. And just underneath the watery blanket looked like something out of a science fiction movie. Like hundreds of monsters about 30 to 40 foot wide gliding next to each other underneath the surface, causing the top layer of water to lift up and constantly change its shape. The water didn't seem to be traveling with the wave; more like the monsters were traveling underneath it, constantly changing the peak of the wave. The peak would hold true for a couple of seconds then either disappear or move to a new location on the swell.

Every time the Intruder went over a wave from the back and we rode down the face of the swell. The boat looked like it was about to pearl or go nose under the back of the next wave in front of us. At the last second, the nose would ride back up the backside of the swell and repeat the whole process of almost pearling the whole way to Bermuda. That is whenever we weren't punching it really fast and doing our customary free fall with just the last foot or two of the backend boat in the water (this was really fun).

Sometime during the second night, we discovered our 3rd ship on the voyage across. This was the closest ship to us. It was within a mile from us, we guessed it was some type of cargo vessel. Ralph thought that he made it change its course because he believed we were heading for the same spot in the middle of the ocean. I'm not quite so sure; anyway, we never got much closer to it. But you have to remember, Ralph can't see without his glasses, and he had a thick layer of salt on the one pair, he could find, of the three he brought with us.

Talk about something spooky, try driving down an eight foot swell into the shadow of itself, with very little light, wondering if the bow of the boat is going to come up instead of plowing under the three foot chop waves between the big swells. Then do it while you're asleep at somewhere between 13 and 25 mph. If that's not interesting, try being the person who's trying to sleep lying down on the freezing bench seat with a good mist of freezing water drenching you every couple of minutes. Remember you don't have much of a pillow and your life jacket is about three inches thick holding your chest off the seat. Your neck is angled at a 45 degree drop to where your head keeps bobbing up and down as the whole boat just about leaves the water, except for a foot or so of the back, before going thud when it hits the water again. Your head is also about three feet away from the Suzuki 115 that's constantly changing its sounds as it revved up and down depending on how much of it is in the water. Now that you have a good picture in your head, try repeating it for about eight to ten hours during the night.

After 12:00, the sea was still giving us a lot of waves over six feet. At night, we usually drove with the front floodlight turned off, because of the glare reflected back off the front deck. When we were wide-awake, we could usually make out the big waves, because of the white chop on top of it, the wind was still howling. But when we were really tired, we pretty much drove blind. We never slowed down, I felt like I was driving a cigarette boat on Miami Vice, skimming along at a high rate of speed. The motor revving up and down, depending on how much of it was in the water.

There was the constant banging of the boat going over the waves. The big bang as we went over the wave, then usually three little ones while we bounced over the chop between the waves. Sometimes, I felt like Whiley Coyote who was just handed an anvil by the Roadrunner. The steering wheel was yanked downward with the unexpected drop going over a large wave. My heels felt like they had small bone bruises, because I was usually barefoot and the boat never stopped thumping. We decided on the return leg, we were going to get some sort of pad to put on the floor. We often sat in the captain's chair and put our feet on one of the three smaller coolers used to store our misc items, food or flare guns. We stored two of the coolers under the chair and one along the side of the chair. I preferred to stand at night. It was easier to stay awake.

Up to this time, we had lost the videos from the two remotes and we were relying on the one hand held video camera. We had a lot of footage of the trip, especially since we moved the camera to the upper cabinet, where we kept the Sat phone and other electronics. We had some really cool sunsets, big wave riding, and some really neat 360 degree pans of nothing but open water. During our last night of the first leg, we decided to keep the camera in its bag in the zipper canvas storage directly over the captain's seat. We did this because we were worried we might have some other valuable equipment fall out while we kept opening the cabinet. We also stored Ralph's telephone pad and other lighter stuff up there.

We're not sure, exactly what happened, either we didn't zip the storage compartment shut all the way, or that the zipper just opened from the camera bouncing up and down going over the waves. Anyway, Ralph was surprised when all of sudden something hit him on the head and bounced into the Atlantic. He yelled that the camera just fell into the water. I turned the boat around as fast as I could, looking for our track in the water. It was disappearing rapidly. The case was dark brown or black. Anyway, it was gone. We lost several hours of video and no way to record any more. We had already spent an hour splicing wires; trying to recharge the batteries from the remote cameras without any luck. They were done. I still had my Gopro surf camera that I shot several pictures, and Jill's old digital camera. I didn't use it because it was stored in my cooler where I thought I was storing my dry clothes, loosely stored in one plastic kitchen storage bag. Actually everything was either under water or floating in four inches of water in the cooler. Lucky for me, I had put the camera in the one Ziploc plastic bag that I used to keep my wallet and passport in.

All of a sudden, the GPS started acting weird. Then the screen just went blank. We tapped lightly on it and nothing happened. Pushing in the plug into the lighter, we noticed that it was really hot, but it wouldn't energize back up. Ralph wiped out some of the excess the grease used to protect the connection from the salt water. We eventually cut off the plug and reconnected the plug from the useless mug warmer. After a few minutes, Ralph deduced that it was recharging. He loaded up the hand held GPS and punched in the coordinates. About a half hour later, it went dead also, Ralph replaced the four double A's and it came back on. Before the next set of batteries failed, the mounted GPS fired up on its own, with all the correct coordinated already displayed.

I have to admit, the weather and waves never scared me, but when we lost the GPS, I was a little concerned because we were still about 150 miles from Ralph's coordinates in Bermuda and about 520 miles SE of North Carolina. We still had the compass and we knew the heading, but the hand held GPS ate the batteries up in less than a half an hour. If we were to rely on it, we'd need to use the compass and then turn on the GPS every hour or so to check on heading. By this time, I knew Bermuda was just a speck in the ocean and we could really easily just go right on by it. We need to know the distance to calculate how long it would take to get there in the event we passed it by. But we still had the Sat phone and could call Harbour Radio in Bermuda (they kept track of all ships entering Bermudian waters), but I doubted that they could pick us up on radar and give us a heading back. We might have to rely on boats, but so far, we only saw three, maybe there would be a bunch around Bermuda.

We called Harbour Radio by sat phone when we were still more than 100 miles from Ralph's coordinates that he got off a GPS street map. He just guesstimated a spot a couple of miles off the SW corner of the island. They gave us new coordinates that were on the NW corner of the island, but we never knew exactly, because we didn't have a chart with us. Anyway, I didn't want Ralph to mess with the good GPS while we were still out of visual from land. He entered them in the hand held GPS, but we kept our heading to the original numbers. We decided that we would call them when we arrived at our first set of numbers. I had no idea of anything; I didn't even know how to set up a GPS, let along, what the shape of the island was.

The last day (Wednesday, May 2nd, third day at sea), as we watched the miles finally go down to double digits, we found ourselves watching the mileage more often and it almost seemed to be slowing down as our speed increased. The mileage numbers that we looked at was the distance remaining, not the distance that we traveled. We knew we were zigzagging and the distance traveled would record that. The fuel was still looking good. The seas had calmed down to three to five with a 15 mph wind. Ralph still making phone calls, many to his wife Anne and his oldest boy Phillip; who had flown to the island to take video of our arrival coming through the Cut at St George, Bermuda. The Cut was the main channel entering Bermuda; it was where all ships had to enter in order to clear customs before doing anything on the islands.

We kept changing our arrival time. Anne wanted to know as close to actual time, since the bus route stopped about 2 miles away from the spot Ralph picked for them. He wanted them to video from the north side of the Cut, a location he got from a map before our departure.

We thought briefly about trolling now that we were almost there, but we weren't sure if we were allowed to catch fish in the Bermuda waters without a fishing license. Besides now that we more or less gave Anne a time when we thought we would be arriving, we didn't want to be late.

Chapter 5
In Site of Land

Around 30 miles from Ralph's Bermuda coordinates; we heard the hand held radio squawk, but with all the boat noise, I wasn't sure of what I heard. Ralph was holding it when it came on the second time. He heard the word Intruder, and answered back. It obvious that they couldn't hear us, we are too far away. Our range was line of site, maybe five to seven miles. Ralph finally called them on the Sat phone, when we're almost to Ralph's end numbers. The numbers that they gave us earlier were on the northwest corner, the other side of the island. They gave us a new set of numbers to a spot about 19 miles away. We continue to the first set of numbers, since I was sure, we should be seeing land any second. My plan was to follow the Eastern side of the island after we spotted shore. We were going to stay off shore far enough to avoid hitting any reefs, no problem, since we are only drafting about 6 inches and the reefs would be visible by waves breaking on them.

After reaching the first numbers and still no sight of land, I started to wonder where Ralph had got these numbers. The visibility was probably no more than a mile or two because of all the salt spray in the air. It looked like we were in the eye of a storm, where we could see short distances in all directions toward the horizon, all that we saw were what resembled fog or a cloud bank sitting right on the surface of the water 360 degrees around us. We had to wipe off our sunglasses every ten minutes or so, the problem was that everything was either wet or salty. Ralph said he just picked the coordinates off the SW corner of the island on a map just a little ways off shore. The coordinates that they gave us had us heading northeast. Soon we saw land, it looked like an opening and I thought it was the Cut that Ralph had mentioned, since I had never seen it on a map or anything. I thought we were only about a half an hour from where we should be able to see Anne and Phillip. I was wondering why we still had many miles to go. The closer we got to the island, I noticed we were drifting off the GPS course, but wasn't worried; we were back to the original plan of following the coast until we came to the Cut.

Ralph called the Harbour Radio and they asked us our location. We told them our present coordinates which put us a little more than a 200 yards from the beach and they all got mad at us and lectured us about the reefs and that we were supposed to stay at least a mile from shore. They gave us a new reading, sending us further north and a little further out to sea. Ralph wanted to explain to them about our boat, but I calmed him down and suggested that he answer yes sir to all their suggestions. They seemed to be really ticked.

When we reached the invisible mark, Ralph was starting to get really steamed; he had been talking to Anne on the sat phone. She wanted to know what was taking so long. She could see us after we described our location using a jet-plane that just flew over us. We were instructed to go to some new coordinates. We had to ask them to repeat the coordinated because the paper we were trying to write them on was wet and tearing. Ralph also was having a tough time entering the numbers on the GPS because his glasses were at first misplaced, then when he found them; they were wet and covered with salt. The new numbers would send us another three miles out to sea according to our hand held GPS. Now we were both ticked, these guys made us feel like they were playing with us. We had no idea, what made them so mad at us. We were in a small 21- foot flats boat that drew about six inches of water. Why did they want us to go further out to sea? We could see the Cut, just a little north and to the west. We felt they were treating us like we were some sort of huge cargo-ship. Ralph protested to the Harbour Radio on the hand held vhf radio while trying to talk to Anne on the Sat phone. Ralph was telling Anne that we had no control of anything. We had to do exactly what they told us to do, even if it was stupid.

After arriving at the mark, they told us to go to another mark, some buoy called the spit buoy. I had no idea of what spit was, I was looking for something on land, or near it. We saw a buoy off in the distance and started to head for it. While closing in on it, we noticed that the GPS was telling us; we were heading in the wrong direction. We adjusted and continued until we found the buoy on the right coordinates. While there, we call the Harbour Radio, and told them our position. They said something about us being at the sea buoy, not the spit buoy. Anyway, they gave us new coordinates. They still seemed agitated at us. I had a hard time understanding them with the poor quality of Ralph's hand held radio and their British accents.

Ralph still had a few more phone calls to Anne, who said that she had to leave, the sun was too hot. Anne had to walk two miles to the bus stop. Phillip was going to stay at the Cut to take the videos. When we finally arrived at the spit buoy; we circled on the spot. It seemed that Harbour Radio got upset if we were even a few feet from the numbers. They gave us some new numbers, and also told us the compass heading. Instead of waiting for Ralph to punch in the numbers, we were writing on the wet paper. I headed in the direction of the compass reading. They called us about 30 seconds later, saying we were heading in the wrong direction and gave us the coordinates again. Now, I know I'm not a very nautical person, but I did know how to read a compass, how could we be going in the wrong direction. We turned 180 degrees and found our selves going to the next set of buoys. Arriving there, we stopped and gave them our coordinates. They said to proceed to the next set of buoys. Well that was interesting, there were buoys going in two directions. I picked the wrong ones again. They could have been a little more helpful. Both of us steaming, we said "yes, sir" and "please" many times in an effort not to tick them off any more.

We could see Phillip, filming on the north end of the Cut. We were finally going to be able to dock. Idling along the center of the channel, lined with buoys, we headed in while asking Harbour Radio for directions to the custom's office. It was located on a small island with a brown wooden sailing ship up on land. We finally managed to be heading for the dock. I was driving, and not used to parking this boat, every boat is a little different, I was a little nervous. I remember when I had a boat, everyone seemed nervous whenever they tried to dock it; often bumping into the dock a little two hard. That's exactly what I did. All the way over, I never had to put the boat in reverse and didn't quite know how much throttle to give the boat. Ralph looked at me, like where did you get your license to drive, but didn't say anything. I told him to finish docking it, since we weren't really ready anyway. The ropes weren't ready, the fishing poles off the back corners were in the way, we almost broke one off, but I grabbed it just in time and stowed it in the rod holder on top of the T-top. We tied up and climbed up on the dock.

The Intruder One tied up to the Bermuda dock at Customs. I'm wearing my long sleeve Ron Jon surf rash guard to protect myself from the sun.

Chapter 6
Customs

Phillip came running along the docks, heading in our direction. We yelled for him to stop. We thought that we would get in trouble, because Ralph had read somewhere that we weren't allowed to talk to anyone until we cleared Customs. The officer on duty said it was OK for Phillip to come and meet us. A few minutes later, while we were inside finishing our paper work, Anne showed up, and offered to go and get us some sandwiches. We were starved, and welcomed the idea of lunch.

Ralph with two Custom's officials and Anne checking out the Intruder, just before Anne went for sandwiches, that were great!

People were gathering quickly outside, they couldn't believe we came all the way from the states. They kept asking us the same questions: Where did you come from? Atlantic Beach, North Carolina, USA. How much fuel did you have? 288-gallons of gasoline. How much fuel did you use and how much is left? We used about 230-gallons and we had somewhere in the neighborhood of 50 gallons left. How long did it take? It took us about 51 hours, but we wasted several hours idling while Ralph talked on the phone, and we've been within a few miles of Bermuda, trying to get to shore for several hours. How rough were the seas and strong was the wind? Seas were three to six with a few hours of eight and maybe a bit larger. The wind was anywhere from 10 to 35 mph. Did you catch any fish? No, we trolled, but traveling so fast, we broke all the rigs that we tried. What kinds of food did you eat? Can fruit, oranges, chips, carrots, crackers, granola bars and cereals. How fast did you travel? 13 to 28 mph depending on how much weight was in the boat. Once the fuel was used up, we picked up speed. We kept the motor at about 4200 rpm. Did any wavebreak over the bow? Yes, we counted five, but only two hit the windshield. Did you guys get seasick? No. Did you take any sea sick pills? I took one, leaving North Carolina. Ralph didn't take any. Did the boat ever fill up with water? Not completely. Did all your stuff get wet? Yes, we needed to bring Ziplocs and train Ralph to lock both sides of all the water-resistant storage hatches. Did you have any trouble finding Bermuda? No, once the GPS was programmed, we just went where it said to go.

In the building, we met one of the Harbour Radio guys that we had talked to on the vhf radios. He came down to check us out. At first, he seemed really business like and a little concerned about us. He tried to find out about our navigational stuff and why we had so much trouble coming into Bermuda. He said we were driving in circles, not going to the right coordinates, not following the right directions, going to the wrong buoys and wanted to know if we had a chart of the waters around Bermuda? We tried to explain everything and admitted to not having a chart. He started to become nicer and after a while, even offered to help us with our weather reports before continuing our journey, which he didn't recommend. He told us that we were very lucky and should seek another way to go home.

Several people had cameras and took lots of pictures, including the officers from Customs. They said that someone from the newspaper was coming down to talk to us, and if we didn't want to wait, they would find us at our hotel, The Grotto. Ralph decided this was way more important, so we waited while Anne came back with the sandwiches.

Eventually, some guy, we first thought was from the paper came by and was taking a lot of pictures. He was dressed fairly well, compared with everyone else on the island. We asked him if he was from the paper. He said no. Then Ralph asked him if he was from the government, and he said no again. He started asking us all about the trip, but Ralph kept giving him the eye. He felt something was wrong. He asked the guy again, and he said no, that he was just an interested spectator. A few minutes later, Ralph asked him again, looking him straight in the face. Are you from the government, and he finally admitted that he was from the Harbour Radio Station. He said they came down to check the boat and us out. He said that we were very disoriented and confused when trying to enter the country. That we didn't follow the coordinates they gave us. We drove around in circles and went the wrong directions many times. We went way further out to sea then we had to go. We argued that we were going to the coordinates that they gave us, or were following a compass reading that they wanted us to follow. Why did we have to go out to sea, when the boat only drew six inches of water? Why did they treat us like an ocean-liner or cruise-ship? What did we do to tick them off? Were they laughing at our expense? He denied everything, saying that they listened to the taped recordings of our conversations and we didn't seem right to them. They wanted to know if we knew how to read a chart. Most of the people that buy navigational charts, buy them to keep from running aground. We told them that we didn't have a chart, the boat only drew six inches of water and that we knew how to visually locate of a reef, especially if there was a swell.

Everyone in authority seemed to want to check out the boat. They all thought it was a bad idea to try to go back to the states. They suggested that we have the boat shipped back, and fly home. You guys were incredibly lucky. Ralph was starting to worry about someone impounding his boat, so that we couldn't make the return trip to New York City. Ralph asked me, if I was willing to just fuel up and head back out to sea? I said, "I'm game." But Anne stepped in and said no way, that we both needed a good night sleep.

Hanging around the Custom's dock, we eventually doubted that the newspaper was even called. We decided to go to the Grotto Hotel and get cleaned up. Anne wanted to go out to dinner in the town of Hamilton. Phillip wanted to drive the boat to the hotel. So we untied the boat and headed around Ordinance Island where Customs was located. We idled for about ten minutes down Ferry Reach until just passed the airport where we crossed a small bay with numerous boats anchored. Phillip motored up to a large complex located on a small white sandy beach. The multiple buildings were three stories tall with peach walls and bright white roofs laid out on an elevation changing plot of land. We had arrived at the Grotto Bay Hotel. We were at one of those tropical postcard locations.

We got permission to tie up to the long cement dock, next to the Triangle Dive Shop located on the property. The guys there were great, especially after finding out about our trip. They spent quite a bit of time learning about our trip and asking questions about ordering a large version of the same boat. They thought it would make a great dive boat. They even talked about the possibility of being a dealer, but just hypothetically.

I couldn't help but notice how beautiful this island was, the water was turquoise and crystal clear. Almost all the homes had freshly painted white cement roofs, the outside walls painted with tropical colors, pinks, corals, yellows, blues, teals and a few whites. Because Bermuda was really an island volcano, the roads and houses followed the contour of the island, going up and down along the cliffs. It reminded me of the pictures I've scene of Greece.

I gave Ralph the combination surfboard lock that was about ten feet of quarter inch cable with a memory curl in it to make it really small. He locked the steering wheel by weaving the cable around the T-top framework and the steering wheel. Spiderman would have been proud. We carried all the stuff up to our room, which was a really long walk, up hills and then up three sets of stairs. We got cleaned up and went to start a couple of loads of laundry. There were only two washers for the whole complex, located way up on the hill on the opposite side of Grotto Bay. We had to wait a few minutes for the guy ahead of us to finish before we overloaded the washers.

Phillip and I walked down to the pool and took a swim while waiting for Ralph to come down and join us. The bartender near the pool, at the Grotto called me over and asked if I was one of the brothers with the boat. He wanted to hear first hand about our trip and bought me a soda, when Ralph arrived, he bought Ralph one too. Everyone here was really nice to us and the surroundings were really beautiful. Phillip told me about the underground caves at the Grotto, and said they were really cool. I wanted to check them out, but I was always so busy I never got around to going down, even though I walked right by the entrance many times.

I decided to let Ralph and his family all go out to dinner while I stayed back to finish the wash and start writing in my journal. Because my shoes were still soaked, I walked around barefoot, wishing I had brought a pair of flip-flops. Most of the grounds around here had sharp rocks in the pavement.

Eventually I ended up writing on the dock by the Intruder. It was chilly, but was also so beautiful. I watched the sun go down, before going back to the laundry, which was just finishing the drying cycle, as I had timed it. But because it was so over loaded, everything was still damp. I went up to the office and bought two plastic tokens for $3.00 each. Laundry is expensive in Bermuda. After the second drying, the laundry was still slightly damp. There were people waiting to use the dryer, so I carried everything back to the room. It took two trips, with everything wrapped up in a large beach towel. The dry items, I folded and put away, leaving Ralph's and Anne's stuff on the bed. Anything damp, I hung around the room, on every conceivable hook I could find and then went for a walk around the Grotto, still in my bare feet. I called Jill, to tell her I made it safely, finding no one home; I left a message on the answering machine.

Ralph and Anne were dealing with the clerks in the hotel lobby; they wanted to charge us 48 dollars for Ralph and me to stay in the same room with Anne and Phillip. Also, they were going to charge us an additional 185 dollars to park the boat at their dock for the night. They agreed to wave the $48, and said we could tie the boat to a buoy, for free, instead of leaving it at the dock. Ralph agreed to pay the $185, he wanted the boat to be accessible and also for security, there were security guards at the Grotto.

We watched Phillip's video tape of our arrival on the viewfinder. Everything looked good until we got to the part of everyone at customs. The tape skipped to the underground caves. Phillip had mistakenly taped over the customs part of the tap. At least we got our arrival recorded, the only part we really needed.

(Thursday, May 3rd second day ashore)

Anne and Phillip were leaving to go to the airport at 8:30 in the morning. They had to be at the airport by 9:00, for a 12:00 flight. We walked them up to the front, where the bellman, which had already heard about the trip via gossip started by Anne and Phillip earlier during the week, told us about the article and the color picture in the paper entitled "The Suicide Challenge". After that, almost everyone on the island knew about us.

<u>Newspaper Article</u>

From: The Royal Gazette (in Bermuda) by Sam Strangeways (published May 3, 2007)

'Suicide Challenge' boatsmen warned about trip to NY

Two brothers who arrived in Bermuda yesterday afternoon after crossing the Atlantic for North Carolina in a tiny open-topped boat were warned last night of the dangers of heading back out to sea.

Ralph and Bob Brown are aiming to set a new world record for the longest unescorted oceanic crossing in a small shallow vessel known as a flats boat. They arrived safely in St. George's at 1:30 pm. yesterday after setting out from Atlantic Beach, North Carolina on Monday morning.

The pair – who have dubbed their voyage the Ultimate Bermuda Suicide Challenge – plan to get to New York by Friday morning, having covered 1,400 miles of open ocean and used almost 300 gallons of fuel in their self-built 21 ft motor boat.

But a spokesman for Bermuda Maritime Operations Centre told The Royal Gazette last night: "We are very concerned about an open boat being in the ocean and the associated dangers with it getting swamped or even overturned in large seas."

"As seaworthy as the boat may be, when all is said and done it's an open boat. In large seas it could very well be overwhelmed. A boat like that shouldn't be out in the open ocean. It's very high risk."

Ralph Brown began designing Intruder 21 seven years ago and has since spent more than a million dollars trying to perfect the vessel. On his internet blog he describes it as "the world's most seaworthy flats boat" and says his seven-day trip is aimed at proving just that.

A post left on the blog on Tuesday says that the brothers experienced five-foot waves on the crossing to the Island. "We received a satellite phone call from Ralph and as of 12:30 in the afternoon, they were halfway to Bermuda," writes a friend called Paul. "sounding pretty exhausted on the phone, Ralph still maintained an amazing attitude."

The post goes on: "He says it's very choppy. Because it's so rough, cooking food really hasn't been an option but he says they're ok. They have been snacking a lot. At night they take little naps on two hour shifts.

"He says that everything is wet, so they pretty much wrap up in some rain gear and try to get a little rest. They lost some of their video feed and equipment and are catching lots of squid. The best news: the boat is running very well."

The brothers were believed to be staying in a hotel on the Island last night but could not be contacted for comment. They are expected to leave for New York this afternoon.

Ralph called The Royal Gazette and they gave him Tim Smith's number, another reporter. Ralph wanted to talk to someone because the article written said that we could not be reached for comment. Sam Strangeways was the reporter that wrote the first article and probably was busy with other stories.

Tim Smith wanted to meet with us in about a half an hour. We had just enough time to buy a couple of papers, walk up to the post office and mail the articles to Ralph's friend Paul in the states. We met the nicest lady who'd been working at the Post office for the past 20 years. She had to really work hard to have Ralph let her do him a favor and save a little on the postage. By cutting two opposite corners of the envelope, so the inspectors could look into the envelope and writing 'local' on the outside. She was able to save Ralph a little. Ralph could hardly resist the urge to pay full price thinking that somehow it wouldn't be delivered. She joked about letting her do what she does and she wouldn't try to design any boats.

Just before Tim arrived, we ran into one of the Harbour Patrol Radiomen in the lobby of Grotto Bay. He wanted to set up an appointment with us to meet with some officials to answer some questions about the safety of returning to the States in the Intruder. We had an appointment for 11:30. Ralph kept saying, "Something's not right! They are going to try to stop us."

Tim Smith, from the Royal Gazette, met us in the lobby carrying his moped helmet and a small yellow pad. He sat down for a couple of minutes scribing in shorthand as we talked. Wanting to get a look at the boat, he asked us if we could continue down at the dock.

Tim looked like he was in his twenties and was really interested in this story. Tim was all smiles as we continued our interview. We were about done, when the photographer called Tim on his cell phone. Finding our location on the Grotto's property; he was on the dock in minutes. The photographer took no less than ten pictures for all sorts of angles. He had a wide angle lens that made it possible to get everything without us having to untie the boat. When he was done, he shook our hands congratulating us on our completion of our first leg; telling us to be safe and good luck. This all felt really strange to me, I still felt like what we did wasn't so special, and yes, I liked the attention. I tried to stay a little to the side and let Ralph take control of most of the conversations. He was really having fun. He had waited along time for this day.

We had about ten minutes before we were supposed to meet with the Harbour Radio group and we still had to check out of the Grotto to look for cheaper accommodations. Check out time was at 11:00 and we were already 20 minutes late. We ran up to the front desk in the lobby to see about getting a time extension. They said they couldn't because they would have to pay the maid service overtime. But they did say that we could leave our stuff with maintenance, and that they could bring it out to the boat with the golf cart. I ran back to the room to start repacking, most of my stuff was still hanging out drying from the night before. I just shoved everything in my bags and was just running out of the room when Ralph arrived. He thought that he could get the rest of the stuff and we agreed to meet at the boat. I didn't want to be late for the group coming to meet us, so I cut between the buildings and hustled along the grass in front of the lower units arriving behind the dive shop.

It was 11:35 by my watch when I made it to the boat. No one was there except for the dive shop people. I loaded the boat and then waited for Ralph to show up. While he was loading the boat, I asked the dive master if anyone had been down at the boat. He said, just before I arrived someone was here and left. That's when I asked him the time and discovered my watch was about ten minutes slow. The dive master received a phone call from the lobby, with a message telling us to wait at the dock. The officials were on their way down to the dock.

We shook hand with the same two radio guys from customs. A lady from the U.S. Consulate, her assistant, a Federal Guy with dark sunglasses, a guy dressed similar to the U.S. Coast Guard and two members of the Bermuda Harbour Search and Rescue Coordinators. We signed some privacy act wavers and gave them a list of our next of kin. They wanted a detailed description of all our safety equipment. Then they spent a great deal of time educating us on the seriousness of the Northern Atlantic. They gave us a series of scenarios to see how we would handle them. How our self-bailing system worked? How we planned to re-right the boat if it tipped over? When we would use sea anchors? If we needed help, the use of flares.... etc.

Ralph had obviously studied up before, because he seemed to basically have good answers. Although, they still shook their heads in disbelief. Ralph was always on the defensive, still thinking this was some kind of ploy to find a way to impound the boat so we'd not be able to complete the trip. Ralph actually asked them if they were looking for some kind of loop hold to trip us up so that they could prevent us from making the trip. They all said that they weren't trying to prevent us, just trying to discourage us.

Bermudian Inspectors talking to us about the dangers of completing our last leg to New York. The Intruder One is in the water behind us.

When they left, everything seemed to be good. They all wished us well and said that they would be dropping off some weather carts to help us pick the right time to depart. They explained that they were really just interested in our safety. They asked us, if we could call Harbour Radio before we left and also to call them every 6 hours, so they could track us. We were too small to track on radar. I think they mainly came by to see the boat for themselves and to meet us. In reality, it was good that they came by. We learned a little and they learned how dedicated Ralph is to completing his mission.

Chapter 7
In Bermuda

Now it was time to leave the boat at the dock and find something to eat. I hadn't had anything to eat since yesterday at customs, 24 hours ago, when Anne brought us some sandwiches. We walked through the Grotto and a couple of 100 yards to the right along the street until we passed the Swizzler Inn. It was recommended to us as a good place to chill with a sandwich and a drink, by one of the dive masters. He also mentioned the grocery store up the street. We walked about a quarter of a mile and never found the store, so we returned to the Swizzler Inn.

Eating out front on the porch, we had burgers and water. Ten minutes after we sat down, an older gentleman came over and asked us, if we were the ones with the yellow boat in the paper. He talked business for about ten minutes and gave Ralph his card, asking Ralph to contact him later.

After lunch, we went inside to pay our bill when another group of three guys saw Ralph wearing a Buccaneers hat. They talked Bucs for a couple of minutes and somehow found out about our trip. Shocked, they asked us to sit down, we tried to leave but they insisted, so we sat down for over an hour. They bought us several drinks; I had cokes, while Ralph had Oduels or other brands of nonalcoholic beer. They were all interested in the trip, but one guy seemed really interested in the company. We told them all about the trip for about a half an hour until the one guy asked tons of business questions. Ralph was having the time of his life, deep in conversation about his boats. After a while, the other two started to seem disinterest, they were more interested in the adventure not so much in how the company was founded and where it was going. Eventually, Ralph notice the glaze in their eyes, and got a phone number from the possible investor.

Three guys we met because of Ralph's Tampa Bay Bucs hat. They bought us drinks at the Swizzsler Inn after hearing about our trip in the Atlantic. Look at all the business cards hanging from the ceilings.

We said goodbye, we had to get to Hamilton to look for a kid's raft (to sleep on), wire, possibly a cheep video camera or security camera and other stuff. On the bus, we found out some of the better stores from some of the locals. By the time the bus arrived in Hamilton, we thought we had barely enough time to run to Masters, Bermuda's version of a small Walmart. Too late, it was already closed.

We found out about another store, Quorems that was supposed to be open till six. The race was back on. We stopped people in the street to help, but while running down Cemetery Street, we missed an alley that would have taken us really close to the store. Instead of stopping to take a quick look at the detailed deficient map, we managed to run about a mile in the wrong direction. Another wasted effort, so we decided to walk around and try to locate some other stores for the next time we were in the area. The Radio Shack that should have been in the Washington Mall was gone, out of business.

It was starting to get late, so we walked back to the bus station to return to the boat. Just as we climbed on the bus an older couple recognized us as the guys from the yellow boat parked at the dock at Grotto Bay. I think my straw hat or the dreamboat T-shirts might have given us away. The couple had snuck into Grotto to use their beach, probably one of the best beaches on the island. They wanted to know why everyone was looking at our boat earlier today. They hadn't seen the newspaper and hadn't known our story. We gave them the short version while on the bus leaving Hamilton. At their stop, they turned around and wished us good luck on our return leg.

We got off at the Swizzler Inn bus stop and walked back to Grotto Bay. I didn't know that the bus also stopped at Grotto Bay. We walked back down to the dock; Ralph was checking something and while leaning over, his favorite pair of sunglasses fell into the water. The water was really clear, but it was a little deep and it was getting late fast. Ralph said oh well and I thought that if we back this way tomorrow, I'd get a chance to go for a swim. The water was still in the low 70's, sometime in August in warms up to the 80's.

Ralph told me where he thought he had hidden the key and wanted me to warm the engine up. I looked all over, but couldn't find it. It was supposed to be in the small toolbox. I glance through all the other boxes. The key had only the red curly wire attached to the small red clip used as part of the shut off switch. We had purchased a little white and red key floater to put it on. We both looked for a few minutes and then I asked Ralph if he had brought a spare with him. He had taped it underneath someplace with duck tape. We looked for a couple of minutes and found it inside the bottom cabinet on the console. Immediately we attached the floater to it. We figured that the original key must have made it up to our hotel room and somehow got picked up with Anne and Phillips stuff.

We were just about to cast off when Patrick, the security guard stopped by to check out the boat. We asked him if he knew anything about St. George Dinghy and Sports Club. We had gotten the name and telephone number from one of the girls working in the lobby of Grotto Bay. Patrick knew Mr. Oately personally who I believe was in charge of the club. He asked us if we wanted him to call Mr. Oately for us. Meanwhile another guard came by and made small talk about the trip. Patrick called his wife to get Mr. Oately's home phone number, because he said that the number Pat from the Grotto gave me wasn't his home number. It sounded like Mr. Oately was asleep when Patrick handed me the phone. Mr. Oately said we could park the boat along the wall east of the gas station. At least that's what I thought he said.

We said goodbye to Patrick and his friend after they used their flashlights to point out the rough directions to the channel buoys. We headed out across the small bay heading for Ferry Reach, the channel leading to St George's Harbour. It was pitch black out because of the clouds blocking out the moon and stars. Using a hand held flashlight, we could see tons of white mooring buoys but couldn't find the red buoys that were supposed to mark the entrance. I think there had to be a channel leaving from Grotto's dock and we thought Patrick was pointing to the buoys out across the bay. We drove around for quite a while, turning around in dead ends until Ralph insisted it had to be closer to the airport. Ralph was right, the entrance to Ferry Reach started at the outside corner of the airport.

We motored through the channel, under the bridge, around the island that housed the customs building. We headed close to shore looking for the gas station or signs of the Dinghy Club. We finally arrived at the last big building with multiple docks, before the Cut. Ralph asked the people hanging out on a huge red racing sailboat if they knew where the club was? It sounded to Ralph that they knew nothing and weren't interested in helping. We headed back the other way toward the main part of town.

Soon we passed a green bar on the water. One of the customers was yelling for us to come over. He said he was right here when we passed on our way to customs yesterday. He wanted to shake our hands shouting that we must have had the biggest set of kahunas to make a trip like that. (An expression we heard over and over again, everywhere we went.) We drove over to talk for a couple of minutes. We thought he said his name was Cooper, but he corrected us and said something that sounded like Fupper. Well to us, he was going to be Fupper. Fupper went on and on, bringing out more of his friends. He bought us drinks. Fupper was feeling pretty good, he obviously had been here for quite some time.

Ralph was really getting nervous because some of the people leaning over the rail to look down at the boat were smoking. He immediately asked them to step back, which they did once they realized they were peering down over a boat full of gas tanks. We asked them where the Dinghy Club was? Fupper wanted us to stay parked along the wall boarding the bar. He even got the owner or manager to come out, but the owner said because of insurance reasons, we wouldn't be able to park over night. Fupper made a big deal about us being heroes and that the whole town should break out the red carpet for us. The owner said we could moor off a buoy about 50 feet off the dock. Ralph said he didn't want to sleep where everyone would be starring at us. But since, apparently, anyone could tie up to a buoy. We idled down about a hundred yards to one of the unused buoys.

Fupper shaking Bob's hand at the White Horse Bar. Fupper suggested Ocean Sails up the street and Angeleen's for breakfast. The Intruder One was tied up along the wall below Fupper's lit cigarette, hence the need for the "NO SMOKING" sign.

Ralph started talking about making a wavebreak. "What are you talking about?" I asked. Ralph reminded me when I asked him, "What would happen if a big wave hit the Plexiglas windshield?" At the time, he sort of changed the subject; he didn't want me to worry about the possibility of a wave breaking the window and possibly kill one of us with a shard. Anyway, he corrected me saying it was Lexan not Plexiglas windshield and started talking about making a wavebreak out of starboard, a type of hard plastic about a half an inch thick.

Remember that we have no saws, drills, glue, straight edges, etc. This was going to really ugly up the boat. I suggested that we talk to Fupper. He mentioned earlier that he knew a sail-maker. We could see if the sail-maker could make the wavebreak out of sail materials. We untied ourselves and motored back to the "White Horse Bar", which was painted green. Fupper wasn't there anymore, but we talked to some of his friends and they told us the sail shop was just a couple of buildings down the street.

We motored back and slept on the boat. Ralph was stretched out on the back bench seat and was sound asleep in minutes. I was wide awake, I couldn't stop thinking about the tile job that I wasn't able to finish and that Jill was ticked that I was going to miss some of our kids' events. Trying to make a longer bed to sleep on, I stuffed bags next to the bench seat that was only about three and a half feet long, so at least half my body was lying on the same plane. My legs hung out over the void between the seat and the rail. My ankles rested on the rail, while my feet hung over the water. After lying there for over an hour, I moved to the bow where I soon froze, even with the shower curtain for a blanket. Ralph was still snoring away. An hour or so later, I move to the small seat in front of the console. I laid there moving around trying to dodge the two inch bracket that dug into my back from the 70 gallon gas tank. It was about 5:00 am when I finally figured I could rest my head on the gas tank, which was the same level as the seat and run my legs through the framework of the T-top. With my shower curtain I slept till about 9:00 AM and woke up with my legs tingling from lack of circulation.

Chapter 8
The Sail Makers

(Friday, May 4th third day ashore)

Using the tape ruler out of one of Ralph's toolboxes, we figured out the dimensions of the wave-break that we needed. We were going to attach it to the framework of the T-top and use the front cleat to pull it tight.

Last night, Fupper told us where the public docks were for the daytime use, in St George. Just to the left of where the Ferry boats park. Idling over there, some people would raise their hands in the air and shout out praises to us. When we docked about six or seven guys came over to examine the boat and ask us about the trip. Most making comments about them not attempting the crossing in anything smaller that a fifty-foot boat and surely not with only one motor.

Again, some of the spectators were getting really close to the boat with lit cigarettes in their possession. Ralph ripped off a piece of cardboard and using a magic marker made a sign that said 'No Smomking'. He then taped it to the rail of the T-top. I scribbled out the second m and Ralph said, "I'm probably the worse speller around." Ralph suggested that we look for a couple of real 'No Smoking' signs.

The sail shop was only a couple of blocks away, a pink building connected to a cabinet shop. Ocean Sails was on the sign. We explained what we were looking for and Rod said he could do it. They had some super strong PVC cloth that they could make it out of. Ralph made sure that he could finish it today. We were still planning on leaving this afternoon.

After explaining the adventure, neither employee had seen the paper. I showed them yesterday's article from the Gazette that I had in my backpack. Then we asked if they had a paper from today. Ralph wanted to check the damage from the interview yesterday. The paper was on a table in the back of the shop. The article was pretty good with a good size picture of us standing on the bow while docked at the Grotto.

Newspaper Article

From: The Royal Gazette (in Bermuda) by Tim Smith (published May 4, 2007)

'Suicide Challenge' boaters vow to continue crossing

They've been variously described as stupid, crazy and idiots, but two brothers yesterday insisted their voyage across the Atlantic on a tiny open-topped boat was not a suicide mission.

Ralph and Bob Brown's 21 foot flats boat—normally designed for shallow water fishing—was tested to the limit as they trekked nearly 800 miles from North Carolina to Bermuda in an unescorted 51-hour journey.

They arrived in St. George's on Wednesday afternoon to book themselves a place in the Guinness Book of World Records, as nobody before has ever traveled so far in such a vessel.

However, even though the trip has been dubbed The Ultimate Bermuda Suicide Challenge by the pair's publicity team, the daredevils claim the risk factor was minimal.

"People are always saying we're stupid or idiots to do this," said Ralph 48, who built Intruder 21, "but it wasn't our idea to call it a suicide mission.

"People do much more dangerous things than this. Look at those guys serving in Iraq, that's dangerous.

"We had no problems at all. We anticipated going through waves ten to 15 feet and they didn't even come that big."

"People can't comprehend these boats can go through big waves, so we wanted to show it could cross an ocean, and we've done that."

"The suicide run was not the boat—the real suicide is what Bob's doing when he goes home and confronts his wife!"

Bob, a painter, explained he had to step in against the will of wife Jill after Ralph's intended voyage partner "backed out" two days before the journey on the advice of his family.

"I was supposed to be going camping, so I had to call her in my lunch break to let her know there'd been a change of plan," said Bob, 49.

"She never said it was too dangerous. I think she was more concerned that I would be away from the family."

"I had a few butterflies the night before, but the boat ran fine. No sweat."

Ralph said he declined his wife Anne's offer to be his substitute partner.

On the trip over, the brothers, from Florida, averaged 13 mph and used 220 gallons of fuel. They took turns to leave the cockpit and were fastened to the boat by rope when they did.

They are expected to leave the Island for New York in a few days for the second leg of their journey, providing the weather is predictable enough.

Ralph said: "We're not going to set off when there's a front—we're not that crazy."

Ralph, who makes and sells flats boats, said he hopes the completion of the mission will help encourage more people to buy his vessels.

> When the pair arrived on Wednesday, Bermuda Maritime Operations Centre raised concerns about the perils of tackling the ocean in a small open-top boat.
>
> They advised them not to go back out to sea, but the brothers have stressed their determination to continue regardless.
>
> "We were concerned about the size of the craft – it's quite small and quite open as well. We asked them what would happen if it took water on board," said a Maritime spokesman.
>
> "But we can't stop them from going back out: We have chatted about their safety on board and we will make sure we keep an eye on them."

Atmaji, one of the sail makers, worked down in the floor (there was a big hole cut in the floor where he sat and the sewing machine's sewing surface was level with the floor), so the sails could be spread out while he sewed on them. Once he found out that we were heading to New York, Atmaji wanted to know if we could send him a souvenir license plate from New York. Atmaji was from Indonesia and had a fascination for New York. He was really excited when we said sure. Soon he couldn't help himself, he asked for two. We agreed. Ralph left a $100.00 deposit with Rod. Rod guestimated the total bill should be less than 200 dollars. They charged $80.00 an hour and the material was really expensive. "If they could get it done today", Ralph said, "it would be worth it."

Just as we were going out the door, Suzann, the owner's wife came in. We explained our trip and said if they wanted to put their name on the wavebreak and give us a discount, it would be OK with us. We were getting tight with our budget. She looked around and saw a banner already made hanging from the rafters. It was a little smaller than the 28" by 56" dimensions we required. She said, she would talk to Steve, her husband, later when he came in.

Fupper had also mentioned that we should eat at a restaurant called Angeleen's. We were both starved. It was only a couple of doors down. We both ordered western omelets. Halfway through our meal, some how, probably due to Ralph bringing up the topic, everyone inside found out about our trip. The Royal Gazette Newspaper was sold there, so we bought two copies, one for each of us. Charles and Foan, a couple eating on a table to the back of the diner, called over to ask for our autographs. They said that we would be famous. I was shocked, nobody ever asked for my autograph. After all, I didn't feel like I did anything. I just went for a long boat ride. At first he wanted me to sign on the top edge of the paper. I suggested he open the paper and have us sign on our pictures. It occurred to me, that I should probably get a picture of us to record the moment. Charles asked if he could get a copy. I told him I would e-mail him one when I got back to the states. We finished eating and decided to start looking for the Dinghy and Sports Club.

Inside Angeleen's, we signed our first autographs for Charles and Foan on the second newspaper article written about our trip in Bermuda.

We idled over to the place Fupper told us it was located. Still no sign of a gas station, we drove into they yacht basin and asked two people talking on the dock. They said this was the place. I guess I must have heard Mr. Oatley wrong since there really wasn't a gas station here. Ralph asked the guy, Francis where he could have his boat pulled out. Ralph wanted to check the engine mounting bolts, the lower end and possibly change the oil. Earlier he added the half-quart that we burned on the way over. He didn't seem to think that changing the oil was that important, since it really wasn't dirty. But I told him that 700 miles in a boat had to be at least more than equal to 3000 miles in a car. After all, it did take 51 hours to get here. A car cruising at 60 miles an hour for 51 hours is over 3000 miles and who drives 60 on the interstate?

Francis was very helpful and pointed out the direction and then drove his car over to the location about a half mile away. By the time we arrived, he had the owner of the shop, Mark, out by the water. The sign on the building still had the old name on it, 'Bermuda Yacht Service'. The new sign was going to read 'Mark Makee Marine'. They had us tie up along side of another boat, lending us a huge bumper because the rail of the larger boat over hung our boat. They tried to line up a mechanic to change the oil, but said that it would be about an hour and a half before they would have time to haul out the boat.

We left it tied up, while we walked to the gas station and hardware store. We wanted to find out if we could get duty free gas. The duty tax on anything imported in Bermuda was 34 percent. Also, we decided we needed 50 gallons more gas for the trip to New York, a hundred miles further, so we needed to find some gas cans. We found out, that diesel was the only duty free fuel available to boats. But, they did tell us that there was a five percent discount for cash sales, a savings of about 100 dollars on about 300 gallons of gas.

The hardware store only had six red and four yellow five-gallon jury jugs. The yellow was for diesel, but it would be OK to put gas inside if we marked it with magic marker. They offered us a ten percent discount because of our trip. Ralph really wanted all the jugs to be red. They thought that they might have some red ones at their warehouse. We bought some other items and agreed to pick up the jugs before 5:00, when the hardware store closed.

We split up. I was trying to locate some sort of kid's raft we could use for a mattress while Ralph was trying to locate an 8-volt power source to repair the video camera. The best I could come up with was two kids swimming rings. I bought them. We met up at the gas station where the attendant gave me two large six-volt batteries. He said he had them for years and needed to get rid of them. Ralph used to be a television repair man and knew a little about resistors and stuff, so he thought he might be able to convert them to the needed eight volts. We picked up the six quarts of oil and headed back to the boat.

Mark and a few of the guys around hooked up a trailer with hydraulic stanchions made to fit any v-shaped boat. Ralph's Intruder wasn't a v-shaped hull. Mark and Ralph figured out what to do using 2" by 8" boards and after 20 minutes we had the boat out of the water, behind an old red tractor. We drained the water out of the rear plugs, tighten the engine plate without the proper wrenches, those were in Florida. Ralph changed the oil; the mechanic wanted four hundred dollars to change the oil in the upper and lower units and the impeller (water pump). Ralph saw no reason to change out the impeller because they usually go bad from sucking up sand or drying out from lack of use.

Ralph adding the last quart of oil during our oil change at Mark Makee Marine. We madė a bunch of friends around there.

Leaving the boat out of the water, we went back to Ocean Sails to pick up the wavebreak. Steve the owner was in and gave Ralph his hundred dollar deposit back and said that he'd like to donate the wavebreak with his logo and website on it. It was perfect. Ocean Sails had become our first sponsor from Bermuda. We spent the next couple of hours there while Steve and gang looked up the weather forecast. While Ralph and Steve studied the weather, Paul another employee from Ocean Sails drove me around to do some errands. Paul told me about his head on car accident and the time he rode down four stories, when some scaffolding collapsed. He was really lucky to be alive. Paul's arm was the only visible evidence that I could see of his accidents. He didn't have full use of it, but he got along great. He had a great attitude on life; he was always telling stories and making sly comments. He was a lot of fun to talk with.

When Paul and I arrived back, Ralph and Steve informed me, that we were going to have to wait out a front that was coming down from the north. Ralph was also updating his website www.dreamboats.net with text and some pictures that we had copied to a disc in the town drugstore, Robert's.

Going back to the boat, Mark and a group of spectators spent about an hour talking with us while they drank a couple of beers. We were still tinkering with the boat. Mark only charged Ralph $50.00 for all his services in hauling the Intruder in and out of the water. Then when Ralph went to pay him, Mark said it was no-charge, he just wanted to help. Ralph had to force the money on Mark, knowing that Mark still had to pay his employees and that they had spent several hours. The $50.00 was already a deal. They helped us launch the boat back in the water and we headed back to the Dinghy and Sports Club.

We weren't sure of where to park, so we tied up to the inside of the main dock next to the opening to the basin after squeezing past a smaller dingy tied to the end of the dock. Our boat was probably the most identifiable boat for its size in all of Bermuda. Because of its canary yellow color and all our junk hanging from the T-top, it would have gotten looks anyway. And since this was a really small island, everyone just about knew of our trip. A small group of curious spectator swarmed around the boat.

The upstairs area was packed. At first, most of the people had trouble believing we made the crossing in the Intruder. Several people offered us drinks and wanted us to stay on their boats when they found out we had planned to wait out the front on our boat. Ralph wanted to just tie up to a buoy like we did the night before, but he also wanted a secure place where we could leave the boat during the day while we scurried around the island looking for stuff. We registered our stay with Andrew the connoisseur. He was like a really good hotel manager.

Andrew was extremely nice and finding out about our budget problem was able to arrange a discount. We were going to leave the boat at the yacht club during the day, then move to a buoy at night so we wouldn't be sleeping in plain view of everyone around the club.

After we were fed, by a table full of food, there must have been some sort of party earlier, or maybe this was something they do every Friday. We were going to move the boat to the slip that we were assigned to, but everyone said to wait till morning, we didn't have to rush.

I hadn't shaved in five days, and it was suggested that I might want to get cleaned up. The guys there also bought us shower tokens for the showers used by the people staying on their boats at the yacht club. Water is scarce on the island. Most of the water used on the island is collected from rain on the roofs of building. There are underground cisterns that store the water. If they run out, then water has to be shipped in. The token is put in the slot and the water comes on in the shower for a set time or amount of water, I wasn't really sure, cause it just turned off whether I was finished or not.

It wasn't long before Ralph and I were made honorary members of the Dinghy and Sports Club, because of our crossing in the Intruder. Ralph was in total salesman mode; he was a talking machine. Most of the people here seemed to know a lot about boats, because of the details in their questions. Later the mayor of St. George came by and had us autograph our newspaper article and have our pictures taken with her.

Ralph talking to Jeff about his long range goals for Dreamboats Inc. The beer in front of Ralph is a nonalcoholic beer. Jeff was a big help to us.

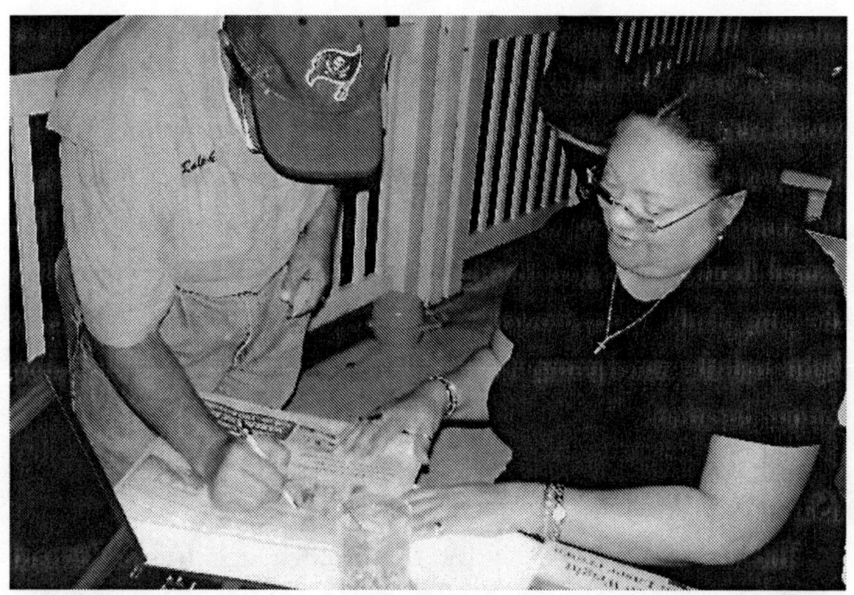

Ralph signing the newspaper article from the Royal Gazette for the Mayor of Saint George on the back upper deck of the Sports and Dinghy Club.

Bob, Brian (member of the club), Mayor and Ralph

After many offers, some from people offering other friend's boats without them knowing; it was agreed that we were staying on Peter Cabral's boat, "The Lady J". He kept his boat moored in the basin. It wasn't very big, but was perfect for us. Its cabin had two beds in the bow and a toilet. He showed us how to set up his gangplank. Peter laid one end on the sea wall and set the other end in what looked like a small football field goal that he set in a fishing rod holder to stabilize the gang plank. Peter showed us the fuse-panel to turn on the interior lights and the water pump for the toilet. We had free use of his cabin for our duration.

(Saturday, May 5th - fourth day ashore)

The next morning, one of the guys from the night before, Richard stopped by to see if we wanted to run up to the Minimark for coffee, a morning ritual. We saw some of the guys I had already met, including Paul from Ocean Sails. When we arrived back at the club, we moved the Intruder over to our spot next to "Inspired Insanity" a 27 foot sailboat piloted by Donna Lange, a 45-ish grandmother who is about to finish her solo-navigational trip around the world. We met her last night at the club and had our picture taken with her.

I was wondering how Jonathan was doing at the track meet, I wasn't sure of the actually times he was racing, but knew by now, he was probably there and warming up to race. There was a one hour time difference between Bermuda and the East Coast of the United States. Bryan was supposed to be participating in an AAU Wrestling tournament and wasn't going to be able to watch his brother run.

While working on the Intruder, we had to rig a long plank that dropped about 5 foot down from the top of the dock. The tide fluctuated about 5 feet, so we had to use about a twelve foot plank which we tied off on the cleat on the cement dock and it sloped down to the Intruder at a steep angle. All the other boats had much higher sides, so their planks weren't so steep. We also spent way more time that it should have taken to run cross lines that would allow the boat to go up and down with the tides. Our main problem was tying a line around the pole that wouldn't slide down the pole into the water, if that happened, and the tide rose, the knot would be under water. Part of our difficulty came from not wanting to cut up all our anchor lines to string these numerous lines so we had a long continuous line going everywhere. Some of the poles had either bolts or shorter pieces of rope that went through the top of the two poles on each side of the boat. The boater could then loop a lasso around the top of the pole and it would not slip down. I felt there was definitely a learning curve for all of this.

The Intruder One docked at the Dinghy Club next to Inspired Insanity with a cruise ship going through the Cut behind. Notice the angle of the gang plank on the front of the Intruder.

We met Eugene, a Bermudian who also has a house in Vero or Melbourne Florida, not much more than an hour away from my house in Merritt Island. He has a small business with a tour train that goes all over the St George Bay. He offered me a free ride at 12:30. Ralph spent most of the day on the computer at Ocean Sails. I decided to start working on my journal. I ate lunch at a restaurant on the bay, right next to the bridge going over to Ordnance Island, where the customs building is located. Eugene's train was supposed to start at the circle there.

The blue and yellow train dubbed "St. George's Olde Towne Railway Tour Train" showed me the town and some of the history of Bermuda. Eugene had me ride up in the front with him and in between his announcements we talked about my trip and about some of the more interesting points of Bermuda. This is where I found out about

Bermuda being the third saltiest place on earth, next to the Dead Sea and the Red Sea. After arriving back at Ordinance Island, Eugene was going to hang out with me and show me some more of the island, but a new group of riders showed up. Among them was a three year old boy that was all excited about the train ride. Eugene went on another tour.

Walking around the square, I found the message board with a notice about the Sunday morning church service. They had what they called "Blessing of the Boats." I guess you were to bring your boat out in front of the public dock across from the custom's dock and have a church service. I'd talk to Ralph later about going.

I bought a cheap kids scuba mask at one of the gift shops, in the square, still hopeful that I might get a chance to take a dip in the water. The nose wasn't even on the inside of the mask, but it was way bigger than a swim goggles but still looked of good quality.

I took the bus to Hamilton and see about a better raft and try to get the video stuff. No luck, so I went to the grocery market and bought the buffet meal. All sold by weight. I had chicken, yellow rice and vegetables, shrimp, and some barbeque all crammed into something about the size of a quart container.

Back at the Dinghy and Sports Club, Ralph was talking to Anne on the sat phone making plans to fly back to Florida tomorrow morning for family reasons. Ralph would be back in three days after the weather front passed. There was also a tropical storm starting up in the Atlantic near North Carolina. We were going to have to wait it out also.

Ralph offered to pay for me to fly home too, but I knew someone had to stay and watch the boat. He also wasn't really financially able to afford it now. I felt that if I was to fly home now, then we should have shipped the boat home when we first arrived, like all the officials wanted us to do and fly home, which would have been great for me. I would had finished the tile job, maybe gotten home in time to watch Bryan's ceremony and for sure seen Jonathan's track meet.

Ralph had always wanted to stay the course; he wanted to finish what he had said he was going to do. The trip was the completed two crossings. He said, "Once you start compromising on what you say you're going to do, your word isn't as good anymore. Dreamboats is going to do what it says it's going to do."

(Sunday, May 6th- fifth day ashore)

Ralph left about 8:30 in the morning, while I was still sleeping. He was going to have to find a bus. When I got up I decided to work on my journal from the captain's seat in the Lady J. I didn't want to take Ralph's boat to the blessing of the boats without him. After about an hour, I heard Donna Lange calling me. I climbed up the plank and walked around the large horseshoe shaped basin to see what she needed. She was covered in grease and smelled like diesel. She was getting frustrated trying to get her engine to crank up. She needed someone to push the started button on the outside of her boat while she bled off the air in her fuel injectors in the engine compartment. We spent about an hour trying to get it started, until her battery wasn't strong enough to crank the motor over with any chance of starting. She'd have to quit until her wind generator recharged her battery. Donna was expecting a mechanic to stop by in a couple of hours.

I spent the rest of the day walking around and working on my journal. The guys at the Dinghy Club were really surprised to find out that Ralph had gone home. One guy comment, "Ralph was chickening out!" He was just teasing. I told him that he could go back with me, but he knew I was just teasing.

I found out that Jonathan had a pretty good day at the State Championship track meet yesterday. He placed 2nd in the 3000 meter and 7th in the 1500 meter. He said that hardly any of the kids ran in both races and that there wasn't enough recovery time between the two races. He also led the 3000 meter race until the last lap, when the other kid passes him in the third turn.

(Monday, May 7th- sixth day ashore)

The next day, it rained the whole day, so I decided to ride the buses and walk a lot of the island. On the way to the store to buy my bus day pass, I stopped by a cell- phone store to inquire about renting a phone to call the states. I thought it would be cheaper than using Ralph's satellite phone. Ralph had prepaid for 500 minutes and we had no idea of how many were left. He used it a lot! I wanted to make a lot more calls. I was surprised at her honesty. She told me that it would not be a good deal and that I should try to get on a computer and use the Internet. There were a few Internet cafés around, one of them being the Ocean Sails shop. I figured I'd get to it later. Mean while, if I had to make a call, I'd just use my own cell phone that I kept off most of the time. I didn't want to have an enormous phone bill when I got back home.

I walked into a couple of gift shops and bought some post card to mail home. I filled them out in front of the post office and mailed them.

I got a phone call on my cell phone from Steve Webster; one of my surf buddies that also happens to be a handyman/carpenter. He said he's been calling my cell phone for the last couple of days and was wondering where I'd gone to? I guess he added a one in front of the number and found me when my phone was left on by accident. He couldn't believe I went on the trip, but then he said it didn't surprise him. He told me to be really careful and he'd see me in a week or so.

I thought of renting a moped, but decided since it was a windy, rainy, ugly day, that it wouldn't be much fun. But I still went into a shop to check on the prices anyway. Not as high as I expected, maybe tomorrow?

I rode the bus to Hamilton and finally was going to make it to Masters. On the way there, I stopped at a paint store to talk about some of their products. At home I'm mainly a house painter. I also wanted to find out if he heard about our trip. I asked him if he heard about the two crazy idiots that came over in the little yellow boat. He did hear about the trip and agreed with me, that they were crazy. He said that they were really lucky that they timed the weather right. I told him, that I was one of them. He was surprised that we hadn't left yet. I told him about the tropical storm off the U.S. coast and he agreed that it was a good idea to wait. I stayed there about fifteen minutes, until there was a break in the rain.

Masters was real close so I jogged there. It was one of those stores that had a little of everything. I found about three types of rafts. I bought the one with plastic handles on the sides because it would be easy to tie to the boat. I found the perfect size 'NO SMOKING' signs that I could stick on the outside frame of the T-Top. I bought a large roll of 3/8" rope, another small water resistant cooler, a couple of cleats and U-bolts that I could use to tie down the ten jury gas jugs.

Afterwards, walked around the docks then decided to ride west. I had never been west of the capital city. With my day pass, I could ride the buses all day, as long as I got off at the end of the line. I think I walked about seven miles at one point, some of it in a pouring down rain. It was scarier walking on the narrow roads with a wall or building right on the edge of the road and nowhere to go when a bus passed you, then on our trip across the ocean. The worse part of walking in the rain along the street was when the cars hit the puddles; you really had nowhere to go. Most of the cars were really nice and slowed down. Oh, and you had to be careful stepping out on the road. The cars drove in the left lane and sometimes I found myself looking in the wrong direction as I was stepping out in front of an oncoming car.

Looking at the pamphlet of the public transportation, I discovered that my bus pass was really a transportation pass and I could use it to ride on the ferries. I decided to ride the bus all the way to the West End, to the Royal Naval Dockyard, then take a ferry back to Hamilton.

I met some older ladies waiting for a ferry at the Dockyard, the very end of the island to the west. We sat there talking for over a half-hour. The ferry must have been closed for the day. It was already 5:30 p.m. One of the buses stopped at the pavilion, a bus stop, that we were waiting at to keep out of the rain. It was heading back toward Hamilton, so we climbed on. We were talking about the journal that I was writing and got on the subjects of books. I told them about how I listen to books on tapes while I paint houses. I told them when I found a good author; I would listen to all their books. I had made the mistake of listening to one of Clive Cussler's books that was abridged and said I'd never do that again. It was way too chopped up. One of the ladies had the Clive Cussler tape that I've been looking for called "Raising the Titanic". The only way I could find it was abridged. She took down my address and said she'd mail it to me.

After arriving at the Hamilton Bus-station, I ran into the same older couple, for the third time at the Hamilton bus-station that snuck into the beach at Grotto Bay. They couldn't believe we kept running into each other at the same spot almost every day. They were also shocked that I hadn't left the island. I told them about the weather. The storm in the Atlantic off of North Carolina was supposedly turning out 30 foot seas in the Gulf Stream. They said, "It's a good thing you waited. Good luck!" (Later I found out that for a short time, the winds were up to 100 mph and the seas up to 50 foot)

(Tuesday, May 8th- seventh day ashore)

The next day, it was really windy. The island even closed some, if not all of the ferries. We were hoping to leave tonight after Ralph returned at 4:00 this afternoon. I walked back up the narrow dirt path that lead up to the driveway then out on the road. Turning around I could see all the boats in the yacht basin. The little intruder was small, but it really stood out. The road took me along the water probably about 50 foot above the bay. Looking toward the bay, I could see the cruise ships docked up by the square, and the many sailboats that have been waiting out the storms on the mooring buoys. The bay was all white-capped with the wind really howling.

I made it down to Ocean Sails to check my e-mail for the first time. I didn't want to tie up their computers. Ralph used them enough for the both of us. While I was there, I sent out an email to most of the people in my address book. Telling them about our trip and why I was doing it. I left so fast, that I didn't tell anyone except for Jill, her parents, Chuck and Vince that I was even going on this trip.

At 2:30 in the afternoon, I came back and went upstairs to the yacht club. This is when I learned that all planes going to Bermuda carry enough fuel to make it back to where they came from in the event it is too windy to land safety. There were hardly any small planes in Bermuda, because they can't carry enough fuel to make the loop.

Since it was white capping in the bay, and some of the ferries weren't running, I started to wonder if Ralph was going to be able to land. I'm sure it was going to be a close call.

I went down and worked on the boat, trying to get things organized. We had bought several small coolers that we could tie up on the back of the captain's seat to make things easier to get to. I tried to turn the 70 gallon gas tank around so that the bracket wouldn't be in the way of our sleeping and we could tie the wavebreak to it. Because of the weight, I transferred several gallons of gas into the other tanks, using the hand transfer pump that didn't work very well. I found that the tank didn't fit because the braces on the bottom were in the way. I turned it back around and looped ropes underneath it. I fastened the wavebreak permanently on by looping rope around the uprights of the T-top through the grommets on the sides of the wavebreak. I ran vertical lines up from the tank to the top forward part of the T-top behind the wavebreak, making the wavebreak form a V. I also connected it to our safety line going to the front cleat.

In some of our earlier conversations, Donna had mentioned that she had an old fashion hand crank drill, that I thought I might borrow to drill some holes to attach the new cleats. Ralph said that I could put holes anywhere I wanted; he'd patch them back in the states. I decided to try to tie them without drilling. I was successful. No need to borrow the drill.

At 4:30, I made the decision to fuel up. Ralph had left me with 2,100 dollars so that we could get the cash discount. The total was $1,967 and some change for the equivalent of 300.5 gallons of regular gas. Several people came up while I spent the hour fueling to either talk or take pictures. One of the bumper buoys, from the Intruder, came loose because of the rope getting cut by the dock. The edge of the cement dock was higher than the Intruder and sometimes in the rough water the thin rope would get scraped. After fueling up, I chased it down next to the shore on foot.

With the weight of the fuel, 338 gallons total. The boat was floating low in the water and the two scuppers (self bailing check valves) which are the three inch pipes going from the lowest area of the deck out the back of the boat with flapper valves on the outside, were below the water level. The flapper valves let water exit the boat and not come in while going forward. They are usually a couple of inches above the water line. Some water started to seep in, but I wasn't worried, the boat was unsinkable.

By the time I got up to the Dinghy and Sports Club. Ralph had already arrived back from the states. He had entered through the front door with a grand entrance. He shouted, "I'm back!" that Donna Lange told me was typical American.

Ralph informed me of the email that he received back in the states from the U.S. Coast Guard.

Respectfully,
Capt Jim Rendon
Chief of Response,
Fifth Coast Guard District

• •

Mr. Ralph Brown
Dream Boats, Inc.

Dear Mr. Brown:

I understand that your company is sponsoring a promotion in which a 21-foot single engine flats boat transited from North Carolina to Bermuda and intends to continue this voyage in the North Atlantic Ocean to New York Harbor. An oceanic crossing in a small craft is highly unadvisable due to the clear danger posed by uncertain weather and sea conditions on the high seas. The severe coastal weather conditions during recent days over the mid-Atlantic have resulted in a number of search and rescue cases requiring assistance. Even in times of fair weather, local conditions can rapidly change with little warning. For these reasons, I am taking this opportunity to advise you that an oceanic crossing of this nature is not recommended.

The Coast Guard has invested significant resources to promote safe boating with the goal to reduce deaths and related boating accidents. Regardless of the outcome, your intended voyage sends a poor message to fellow boaters with regard to safe and responsible boating. While I applaud the communications plan and the operators attention to the weather, there are certainly more responsible ways to prove that your company builds a quality vessel without jeopardizing the lives of those on board and the lives of potential search and rescue responders who would get called upon in time of need. I ask that you reconsider your sailing plans and declare victory from Bermuda while you are still able to do so. I also recommend that you emphasize the importance of boating safety as the primary factor in your decision to forgo a transit to New York. Our desire is to have boaters, both young and old, look to Dream Boats Inc. as company that not only builds safe boats but also promotes safe boating. I am available to discuss this issue with you at your convenience.

Sincerely,
J.E.Rendon
Captain, U.S. Coast Guard
Chief, Response Division
Fifth Coast Guard District

Wow! Ralph is really getting the attention of some really important people. I sure hope the weather predictions hold true. I would really hate to call for help after receiving a letter like that.

Ralph spent the next couple of hours using Donna's laptop since he had made the decision to wait till morning to leave because of a TV interview that he scheduled for our departure, besides it was still really windy. A bunch of the guys came by to say goodbye. Jeff even stopped by to give us a Bermuda chart and me his old spring wet suit. It was long pants with a tank top. He even gave me a pair of booties. He also gave us both a nice lightweight sports jacket, saying that if we got an interview with Matt Lauer from "The Today Show", we needed to look good. We both laughed, but I'm sure Ralph was hopeful.

It was dark by the time we made it out to the boat. We crammed our extra rain ponchos that we never used, in the scuppers to slow the water entering the boat. We cut strips out of the rubber mats that

Ralph brought back from the states. We duck taped them around the jury jugs of gas that I tied up earlier. This way, they wouldn't bounce around and possible chafe causing a leak, even though we still tied them in really good.

We refilled the water jugs. Just as we were about to call it a day, we noticed the port side listing a little lower then the starboard side.

The port bilge was not coming on. There was probably at least 30 gallons of water in the left hull. "I sure hope it's a bad wire connection, I'd hate to go back without all three bilge pumps. We'd probably have a tough time locating a pump early in the morning." Ralph said.

Lucky for us, it was a bad wire connection. The connection from the boat to the bilge pump was below the current water level in the bilge. It was a mess of creamy green slim caused by the salt water due to the extra weight of all the fuel causing the boat to ride lower in the water then normal. Ralph made a note to improve this in his future boats. We replaced it with new wire; only to discover we picked the wrong brown wire to attach it to, the pump ran continuously. We rewired it again to the brown and white wire so that the auto switch would work. We should have cut open the shrink-wrap connection to verify which of the brown wires to use.

Ralph asked me about the food that I bought for the return trip. When I told him I stocked up on the fruit cocktail, he told me about the 6 cans that he had taken away at the airport, because he couldn't carry them in his carry-on. It was 12:00, time for bed. Ralph started snoring as soon as his head hit his bag of clothes he used as a pillow, in the Lady J.

On one of my phone conversations with Jill, I found out that my father in-law had found someone to finish his tile job. I was glade that I didn't have to worry about that any longer. I just wished he'd let me have one of my friends finish the job. It would have been finished within a couple of days after I left and I wouldn't have had so much trouble sleeping on this trip.

Newspaper Article

From: The Royal Gazette (in Bermuda) by Tim Smith (published May 9, 2007)

Brothers set to resume boating record bid

Two brothers are this morning due to resume their "Suicide Challenge" across the Atlantic—against the better wishes of the US Coast Guard and Bermuda Maritime Operations Centre.

Ralph and Bob Brown are hoping to write Records by voyaging from the Island to North Carolina on their tiny open-topped boat Intruder 21. They reached Bermuda last Wednesday on the 21 foot flats boat—normally designed for shallow water fishing—following an unescorted 800 miles trek in the other direction.

Last night, Ralph, 48, thanked the people of Bermuda for their friendliness during their stay on the Island.

"People here have been wonderful. I don't think I have ever been anywhere like it before.

"I've got butterflies in my stomach but everyone does. But once you get out there and get going, it's different."

The trip has been dubbed The Ultimate Bermuda Suicide Challenge by their publicity team, but the Brown brothers insist the risk factor is minimal. Ralph says he hopes the mission will help him prove the seaworthiness of the boat he built himself.

However, a US Coast Guard email to the brother yesterday stated: "Even in times of fair weather, local conditions can rapidly change with little warning. There are certainly more responsible ways to prove that your company builds a quality vessel without jeopardizing the lives of those on board and the lives of potential search and rescue responders who would be called upon in time of need.

"I ask that you reconsider your sailing plans and declare victory from Bermuda while you are still able to do so."

A Bermuda Maritime Operations Centre spokesman said last week: "We were concerned about the size of the craft – it's quite small and quite open as well. We asked them what would happen if it took water on board.

"But we can't stop them from going back out. We have chatted about their safety on board and we will make sure we keep an eye on them."

The Brown brothers, who are from Florida, expect to arrive in North Carolina on Friday morning. (the paper meant to say New York not North Carolina)

Chapter 9
To New York

(Wed May 9th- last day ashore and first day at sea)

We woke up at 5:30 a.m. Ralph all excited about the trip. The Bermuda Broadcasting TV reporter was to meet us at customs. We were going to tow Donna Lange out to the buoy, beyond the reef, after leaving customs. She wasn't ready yet for us to give her a ride to customs. She said customs doesn't open till 8:00. She said that she would walk up there around 7:30 and we could give her a ride back to her boat after we cleared customs. She wanted to work on her diesel engine, hoping it would start, after the batteries were recharged. Donna hadn't had any luck with the mechanic being able to repair her diesel.

We were to meet with the interviewer at 6:30 at customs. He stopped by the Dinghy and Sports Club to make sure we were coming. We told him, we were leaving now and we'd meet with him as planned.

After packing up the last of our stuff that we had in the Lady J, we left Peter a short thank you note and one of Ralph's Dreamboat T-shirts as a souvenir. Ralph and I were really fortunate that we met so many great friends in Bermuda.

Arriving at customs, the interviewer hooked us up with microphones on our shirts. I was a little nervous, but he made us feel at ease. Ralph did most of the talking, and then he asked us just to mill around on the boat for him to get some film that he could later edit. There was still plenty to do, so we just finished stowing things away. This was when Ralph discovered that he was missing his notepad with all his telephone numbers and notes.

Andrew stopped by to say goodbye. We asked him if he had a key to the Dinghy Club, but he didn't, he was on his way to his other job. He said to go back and wait for someone to open it up. Someone had to take the money from the register to the bank and also the janitors would be there soon. The interviewer had us drive away, like we were actually leaving, and we just drove back to the Club since it was just a little past 7:00. We weren't leaving Bermuda till Ralph had his notepad. We figured he must have left it on the table next to Donna's laptop, and someone must have moved it, because Donna said it wasn't there when she came for her laptop last night.

Around 8:00 we took Donna with us to customs. We figured we'd just have to go back to get Donna's boat "Inspired Insanity" anyway after clearing customs. We had the usually commotion at customs; including a captain cutting in line in front of Ralph and me. He said he was in line and had to step out to get something. We didn't believe him, but let him go anyway. He was in some kind of sail boat race was trying to clear all his passengers in and out of Bermuda with only their passports. They were still on his sail boat at the gas station. All they stopped in Bermuda for was the gas station. A few people were checking out our boat. Ralph was offering everyone a ride to New York. He had no takers. Charlie, another friend from the Dinghy and Sports Club, stopped by on his way to work and wished us luck.

The custom's officer gave us back our flare guns, and while I was putting them back in the case inside the cooler with all the other flares, I found the missing boat key. The key was underneath all the red flares.

That must have been why I hadn't noticed the red curly wire and red clip.

As we were driving back to the Dinghy and Sports Club, we saw some of the people from Ocean Sails leaning out of their second story window waving. We pulled by the dock next to the path that went up to their building. Steve came out to the dock and wanted us to come up to get a last minute weather report. He didn't think it was time to depart yet. After taking another look, he agreed that there was indeed a small window. He said it would be a little better if we left on Saturday. Today on Wednesday, the seas might be five to nine foot, but after that they would start shrinking. We decided that as long as the seas were below 12 foot, we were going to go. We took a bunch of pictures and went back down to their dock where another friend called me from Florida.

Crew at Ocean Sails: Ralph, Rod, (parrot), Bob, Steve, Suzanne, Atmaji, a customer and Paul (in front). They made the Wave Break for us; helped with the weather reports and supplied some of the photos.

Tim Golden, one of my surf/motorcycle friends called me. He must have gotten his e-mail about our trip. He had been watching the storm off the Carolinas. Tim said, "Hey you knuckle head, you better not be off shore, you know there's a huge storm out there. The seas out there are over 30 foot!" I told him, that we were still on shore and that the seas have already dropped. We'd be leaving in just a little while. We had just finished checking the weather report just minutes ago. He wished us good luck!

View looking at the fuel on board the Intruder One. (4) 50 gallons on the sides, (1) 70 gallon up front, (10) 5 gallon jury jugs next to the white coolers and the 18 gallons under the console totaling 338 gallons.

Back at the Dinghy Club, we still had to wait for the janitor to come and open up. We could see the white notepad next to the register, behind the counter while looking through the window. I worked on my journal, knowing that once under way with all the water spray and bouncing I wouldn't be able to take notes. Ralph was talking to some of the people down stairs, including some from Ocean Sails. We finally got his notepad and got ready to leave. Steve and several others were taking tons of pictures. Our bilge under the console came on and started pumping out gallons of sea water through the 1 ¼ inch black hose. I asked Steve to get a picture; I thought it was kind of neat looking, just before leaving our boat was still taking on water because the scuppers were below water level.

Some of the other sailors pushed Donna's boat out into the basin, and then using ropes from other boats guided her so we could pull her out to the channel. Once in the channel, we let out some more line and tied her off to the two eyehooks on the transom. The people on shore were taking pictures and waving goodbye. Everyone was wishing both boats good luck.

I'm not sure how Ralph felt, but I felt really special being able to help tow the Inspired Insanity out to sea. We were able to help someone who would probably be in tons of sailing magazines. I couldn't get over the fact that her trip around the world by herself took in the neighborhood of 300 days and we made it possible for her to finish her dream today.

We idled a little and soon stepped up the speed. The Cut was fairly rough due to the waves being so close together. Donna's Inspired Insanity bounced up and down while we crashed through the waves. Steve and Suzanne were snapping pictures to send to Ralph's web master Paul. I was getting a little emotional, or maybe I had a little salt in my eyes. That lump in my throat was probably just because I might have been thirsty.

Halfway through the cut some sort of tourist boat was passing us on our portside. It had about twenty buoys hanging off the sides. We never paid it any attention because we were busy video taping our departure and yelling back and forth with Donna.

The waves in the Cut were small but because they were funneled into the Cut, they came in relatively close together. With the extra drag on the back of the Intruder and our full load of 338 gallons of gas, the Intruder was really low in the water. We were plowing through the waves; water was spitting out the front and blowing every which way. We waved at Steve and Suzanne on the rocks 15 foot above the water at the edge of the north side of the cut. The waves were a lot more intense on the north side and splashing ten foot into the air. I'm sure Steve who was a little further out than Suzanne was getting a little misted.

Just as we exited the mouth of the Town Cut, a two story 40 something foot white catamaran with Black and pink stripes was entering the Cut about 30 feet away from us. Many were waving and probably a little bewildered because of us towing the larger sailboat out. We waved back. It looked really cool from behind, we could see underneath the whole boat, right down the tunnel.

We towed Donna out more than a mile then she rolled out her jib. Soon she was ready for us to cut her loose. Ralph started to try to untie the rope off the eyelet. It was taking too long, so he asked me to hand him his fishing knife. She headed more north easterly, and we headed in a more westerly direction, all the while waving good luck! We were expecting to be in the states in about 60 hours, Donna in about ten days.

We called the Harbour Radio, and they were a little irritated, that we didn't call them before we left the dock. We agreed to call them in four hours instead of the six that we agreed to at our meeting at Grotto Bay. Ralph made his satellite calls off his list taped to the windshield so we wouldn't have to fool around with his notepad. The seas were only about three to five, with 10 to 20 mph winds. We were heading toward the underwater reefs, but they shouldn't be a problem since we had a shallow draft. The water was still clear and we could see the bottom.

Ralph let out a couple of screams, "We're doing it! We're going to New York!" We took turns video taping with another camera that he brought back from Florida. I resisted the urge to have Ralph stop and drift so I'd be able to at least say that I snorkeled in Bermuda.

21 foot Intruder One towing Donna Lang's 27 foot sailboat out past the reefs, so she could finish her solo circumnavigation of the globe. The wind generator is above Donna's head.

It wasn't too long, before Ralph decided he needed to get something out of his dry clothes cooler. We were probably about 50 miles off shore from Bermuda. And wouldn't you know it, with all the fuel plus the added 50 gallons of gas up front. It didn't take long for a rouge wave to completely fill up the boat. It came over the bow with Ralph's extra weight up front. I didn't see it coming, it happened really fast. I was watching Ralph rifle through his things and looked up just as the wall of water splashed over and around him. The boat instantly slowed as the water rushed through the boat, filling it to the rail. Not that the wave was all that big, with all the fuel tanks and coolers on the deck there wasn't much room for the water, it didn't take a lot of volume to top off the boat. Ralph closed his cooler just after a couple of gallons of seawater made it into his cooler. It was a good thing that the hinges were on the forward part of the cooler and that Ralph was forward of the cooler on the bow deck looking over the lid. I don't think Ralph actually closed the lid, rather the wave slammed him flat onto it, closing it in the process. Lucky for him, he had used zip locks to protect all the tapes and stuff, but he never got around to double bagging everything in a large trash bag for extra protection. All the water drained really fast out the large scuppers, and the only thing that happened, was that his cooler was knocked free from the plastic bracket used as a tie down the four corners bolting the cooler to the deck. He reinforced the tie down for the cooler and did mine while he was at it.

The first day was pretty uneventful after the first couple of hours, except for when the engine oil light started blinking. I was driving, everything was going smoothly. Ralph was up front daydreaming of all the things he has to do and enjoying the beautiful overcast day we were having. As I glance down at the GPS for like the thousandth time, I noticed the red light blinking at the bottom of the oil pressure gage on the dash. "Hey, why would the oil light be blinking?" Ralph yelled for me to shut off the motor.

He said his first thought was that he hadn't double-checked the oil level after starting the motor up after the oil change in Bermuda. Ralph said, "I can't believe it could be that low?"

He rigged the sea anchor and he threw it out. He was using a really long line and wasn't impressed with it. The boat was taking a long time to turn into the wind. He shortened the rope and also threw out his home made sea anchor. Together, the boat swung around so that the boat was pointing toward the wind. We pulled the motor cowling off and checked the oil. It was clean and full. I thought, so much for the easy fix. The motor had been running perfectly. I thought, not being a mechanic, I sure hope it's not the oil pump. We didn't change the filter, because we couldn't readily find one in St. George, but the oil was barely discolored, there's no way the filter could be blocked. Ralph then called his mechanic in Florida and after explaining everything we did. Marino told us to call him back in half an hour while he looked it up in the engine manual.

I wanted to see how well the kicker worked. We started it up a couple of times to make sure it was working properly while in S. George. Now for the real test.... I started the six horse power kicker while Ralph pulled up the sea anchors. We looked at each other and said, "Which way should we go?" We were about 70 miles from Bermuda and 700 miles from New York. Going back to Bermuda meant that we would have to go against the current, and also that we would have failed in our first attempt to make it to New York. We both decided that we'd start driving the kicker on our same heading of 330 NW toward New York. We might be a couple more days out here, but what ever happens, happens!

We fooled around with the video camera, making commercials and stating our intentions. We made commercials about our kicker, what to do when your trusty Suzuki 115 wants to take a break. The other one was about our favorite food on a voyage, fruit cocktail with the easy to use pop-top. We had both sent three minute tapes to Jeff Prost of the TV show 'Survivor' several years ago, Ralph made it to one of the interviews. One of the questions they asked was what would you do for a million dollars? We had both sent statements about doing some sort of ocean trip for the million. Anyway, we actually did a trip and thought about sending him a short tape about this one. We never made the commercial, but talked about it a lot.

Meanwhile we discovered we could go about five miles per hour with the kicker and figured that after we burned off most of the fuel, we could eventually maybe get it up to eight or nine mph. We had 700 miles to go to N.Y. at an average speed of seven mph; we'd be there in 100 or so more hours. The good news, we wouldn't have to stop for Ralph's phone calls.

We had agreed that we would use the Suzuki at a lower rpm, giving it rest every hour or so until it blew up, then we'd to use the kicker, we'd wait a while before telling Harbour Radio. Since we weren't planning on going back to Bermuda, all they would have needed to know was that we were all right. Besides, according to Steve from Oceans Sails, the seas were to start calming the next couple of days. The kicker would work.

Soon the half-hour was up and Ralph called his mechanic. Marino said that the light meant it was time to change the oil. And since we just did that, then all we had to do was reset the computer, by turning the key and pulling up on the kill button several times. The kill button is a button that has a removable pin attached to the driver. If the driver got too far away from it, it would shut the motor off. We really should have used it, but never did. Since we were tied to the boat, we didn't feel it was necessary. We barely finished the oil deal when it was time to call Harbour Radio. I was glad we got that cleared up before we had to make our call.

We made our calls every four hours and the seas weren't any bigger than six foot, matter of fact, most of the waves were probably smaller than five foot. The skies were ugly, with clouds blocking out much of the sun. The water had small chop on it, but most of it wasn't white capping. We did have a total of three waves come over the bow with two hitting the wavebreak. We never saw any of them coming.

When the oil light came on, we used the kicker while waiting to hear from Ralph's mechanic Marino. We were still heading for the States. This would have been a good time to fish.

While driving, it became apparent how dumb I really was. After driving all the way to Bermuda and part of the way back, staring at the GPS every couple of minutes, I just realized that we really weren't supposed to try to bring the arrow and the line together. Just steer the boat in the direction that the arrow was pointing. That was the real purpose of the arrow. I guess the GPS manufactures thought they made it idiot proof with the arrow. Well I proved them wrong. Ralph said it really doesn't matter as long as whatever we did gets us there.

When night came, it was pitch-black; there wasn't a moon or stars out. The clouds blocked out everything. We used Ralph's front light most of the time, since he taped a foam shield underneath it to block out most of the glare. But we really were just driving blind. Our main job was to watch the GPS and try not to fall asleep. After a while, Ralph had me calling the Harbour Radio and they started asking lots of questions, probably trying to judge our mental awareness.

Ralph made some of his calls behind the wavebreak if the seas were less than 4 foot and we also found that it wasn't too bad of a place to sleep, if you didn't mind waking up to a Charlie Horse (leg cramp). We didn't see to much sea life while it was choppy except for flying fish, squid, man-o-wars and an occasional fin breaking the surface, probably from a large fish.

Ralph making calls on the Sat phone inside his cubby behind the wave break. Sometimes we slept there.

Somewhere near the halfway point, when we called Harbour Radio, they asked us our fuel situation. I did some quick calculations and told him we had used up about half our gas. He seemed really worried, but I told him, that now that the boat was lighter, we'd be riding on top of the water, and not plowing through it. We would be picking up speed and also getting better fuel economy. After hanging up, I did the math several different ways and always came up, with us having around 30 to 40 gallons to spare. At an average of five gallons an hour, we have six to eight hours of fuel to spare.

On our first leg we averaged 4.5 gallons of fuel every hour: 230 (gallons on our first leg) divided by 51 (hours from North Carolina to Bermuda) = 4.5 gph. So 5 gph we would have an extra half gal of fuel an hour for cushion. 169 (gallons left) divided by 5 (our average fuel consumption) = 33 hours to go. We were averaging at least 18 mph so if we went 33 hours x 18 mph = 594 miles. 594 (miles we could go) minus 387 (miles left to go) = 207 (extra miles).

My other way I did the math: On the trip over we averaged 2.9 mpg. 674 miles divided by 230 gallons = 2.9 mpg we were actually getting much better because we were constantly zigzagging. The half way spot left us with about 387 miles to go. Half of our fuel left us with 169 gallons. We needed to get at least 2.28 mpg and since the boat was constantly getting lighter, our fuel consumption had to be well over 3 mpg on the last half of the fuel. If we averaged 3 mpg on the 169 gallons left, we'd have enough fuel to go 507 miles. That gave us a margin of 120 miles extra.

The first two days, we ate peanut butter and jelly sandwiches, cold cans of baked beans, fruit cocktail, chips, Fig Newton's, crackers and raisins. We finished off the blue Gatorade and then drank water. Every now and then, I started making a wish list of things to eat. I wasn't really ever hungry. We were always munching on something. I can't believe neither of us bought any tootsie pops.

Every now and then I would have time to think about this trip. We were a boat small enough to completely disappear in the trough between two waves. Sometimes I would imagine someone trying to locate us by satellites out in space. They'd first view half the earth, then each time they zoomed into our area out in the Atlantic, all they would see would be water and maybe a cruise or cargo ship. Eventually, they'd zoom so close that we would be visible and I would love to just wave up and smile. According to Ralph, we were doing something that no one on earth has ever done before and to me, it was just a boat ride.

Early in the evening, there were storm clouds building all around us. As far as we could see there were bands of dark cloud. There didn't seem to be any lightning close by, but it was still a little erie being hundreds of miles from shore with nothing but the sea and a sky full of storm clouds. We were lucky for the most part. We managed to just miss the rain most of the time.

We weren't able to experience the sun set due to the fact that we couldn't see the sun all evening. Just as it was becoming dark the night the sky was clearing behind us to the east and we could see tons of stars and a quarter- moon coming out. It was really starting to cool off quick. At least we'd be able to see a little driving at night. Then a bunch of bands came through and the sky was dark again. It started to rain really hard for a while. I was glade when I was too tired to drive and Ralph took over. I wasn't really sure what was worse. Driving when you can hardly keep your eyes open or trying to go to sleep while the ocean continually misted you with its salty refrigerator water.

An hour or so before I relinquished the pilot seat, the seas picked up again. Because it was blackout dark, we had no idea of the size, probably four to six. Ralph took over and the seas stayed rough for most of his shift with a serious downpour. He said it started to calm down about an hour before he woke me up.

Chapter 10
Our Last Day at Sea

(Friday, May 11th- third day at sea)

Ralph woke me up for my shift a couple of hours before sunrise. The seas had calmed down since the last time I drove. Maybe that explains how I had gotten my best sleep of the trip so far. The sky was still dark and starless, but we were cruising near 25 mph. I couldn't see, but it seemed like the swells were down to one to two, with almost no wind. We were making our own wind, by our speed. I would have loved to stop for a minute and put a thermometer into the water, but mine was in my home made Jacuzzi back in Florida. I wondered how long someone could survive floating around out there dressed like we were?

By morning, we were both frozen solid and could hardly wait for the sun to come out of the clouds. I was driving and couldn't stop shivering. I'm sure that when Ralph woke up, he'd be even colder. The sleeper always woke with the shakes. It seemed that the sun was just minutes away, so I got out the camera and started taking some pictures. My self-portraits were taken at arm's length because I didn't want to wake Ralph up. We lost most of the really good video on the first leg of the trip. I wanted to get some good pictures of the sunrise. The sun was coming up, it was behind a bunch of low clouds and just when the sun was about to exit the clouds, we drove past a cloudbank and it blocked out the sun.

I had been calculating our arrival time to New York using our mileage left and the speed we were traveling at. We should be docking sometime around 2:00 p.m. I was hoping that it would be one of those hot sunny days.

An hour or so later, with the gray clouds as a background and everything hazy, Ralph pointed to what he at first thought was a waterspout. But as we got closer, we realized what we were seeing was a group of several whales spouting water and air up at least six feet. He said he saw the dorsal fin and part of the backs. But they disappeared as we drove over to the spot where they were hanging out.

Not long after this, we came across at least 40 large dolphins or perhaps pilot whales; they were gray/black on top and a dirty white underneath. Most were traveling in groups of seven or eight and were spread out over several hundred yards. Many were breaking the surface in what looked like play. We slowed the boat down to about 15 mph and a group came over to the boat. I got really excited. I was hoping that some would play in the wake and bow spray from the boat. While I snapped pictures, Ralph got out his camcorder. In all the excitement, Ralph swung the camcorder back and forth at breakneck speed while I didn't miss a chance to stick my fat head and straw hat right in his lens. They swam in the wake and under the boat up to the bow. Several rolled on one side and looked like they were watching us. While going under the boat they resembled lime green torpedoes until their dark backs broke the surface. They played for several minutes then just disappeared. Wow! That was really cool. I've always wanted to see that. We seriously thought about turning to follow them, but didn't.

Some of the 40-ish white sided dolphins that came around us on our last day at sea. Several came and played in our bow spray and wake.

We had a large bubble of water in the lamp over the cockpit so we stopped to take off the cover and remove the water. The Phillip screws were really small and I thought for sure we were going to loose at least one of the four. We didn't.

I was driving by looking at the GPS, when Ralph noticed that we had two different headings. The compass and the GPS weren't reading the same course. That's when he noticed that we left one of our screwdrivers on the dash next to the compass. When he picked it up, the compass course corrected and matched the GPS. The screwdriver had a magnetic end.

An hour or so later, the GPS went out again. Those lighter plugs were going bad again because of all the salt. The plug was hot and smelled like burning plastic. We decided to hard wire it in. We removed the plug and pulled out the wire from under the console. I spliced the wire directly to the GPS wiring. It still didn't work. Ralph asked me, if I had cut away all the dark copper wire? I hadn't. I scraped it, and then clamped a connector to both wires. He decided to cut away the bad wire; it went all the way to the to the battery box. He ran all new wire and the GPS fired right up. We didn't even have to wait for it to recharge. Lesson learned, no lighter plugs mounted where they get exposure to the elements. Normally, the Intruders don't come equipped with lighter plugs, but if they did, location, location, location. These were mounted for the Bermuda trip only, and he wasn't planning on leaving them on the boat when he arrived back in Florida.

We drove in an almost total whiteout wet fog for a couple of hours. We could barely see more then one length of boat off our bow. We were already freezing and dripping wet since late last night. A couple of hours in damp dripping wet fog wasn't going to dampen our spirits. We were both excited while speeding at a whopping 28 miles per hour since the seas were still under one foot. When the fog lifted, it was back to the same dreary over cast day.

We were about 60 miles off shore when we called Harbour Radio; they commended us on a job well done. We told them we'd call them after we were on shore. At this time, we also called the U.S. coast guard to inform them that we were almost to the Harbor. The Bermuda Harbour Radio was also keeping the U.S. Coast Guard posted of our whereabouts. The Coast Guard gave us a number to call when we arrived so that they could send a boat out for us to clear customs. They warned us of all the wood floating in the Harbor.

When we were about 30 miles off shore, we started noticing all sorts of trash in the water. We assumed that it was from cruise ships, but we really couldn't be sure. Paper and plastic everywhere! A little closer in and we saw our first boat of the day. It was a shrimp boat. Next we noticed some buoys; Ralph thought it might be for a long line, used for fishing. A couple more shrimp boats, some of them waved back, Ralph tried to call one on the radio, with no response.

This was about the time I started secretly fantasizing about the steak dinner that I was going to eat after we met up with our Uncle David. Uncle David was going to meet us on shore. We weren't starving or anything, but I thought that a big T-bone or something would be appropriate for our victory celebration. Besides, taking him out to dinner would be fun. Uncle David was always really interesting to talk to.

We both wanted to be home in Florida for Mothers' Day and decided to leave New York as soon as possible except if by some lucky chance we got invited to be on some sort of talk show. Ralph was really hopeful, but I still had my doubts.

We started to make out the New Jersey coast; Ralph made some more phone calls. Ralph's coordinate numbers were right on this time. We could make out some of the buildings and then we spotted what we thought was the Brooklyn Bridge, (really the Verranzano Narrows), there was a huge container ship approaching it. We soon passed the cargo ship as we closed in on the bridge. It was 3:04 PM when we passed underneath it. That was really cool looking straight up and seeing all the support beams.

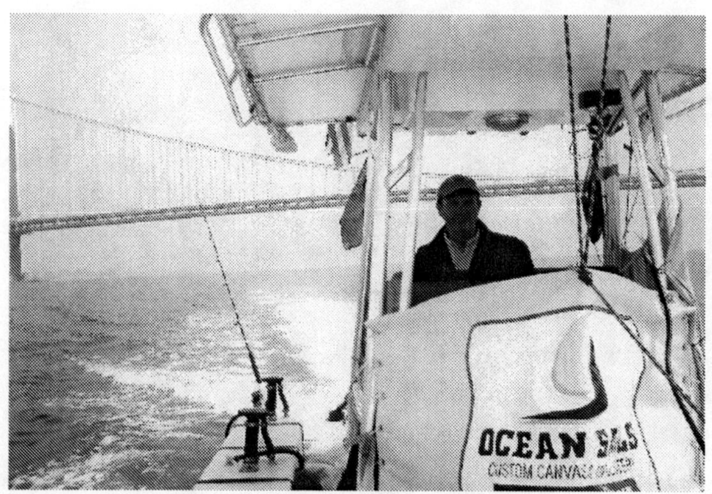

Ralph driving past the Verranzano Narrows Bridge entering the New York Harbor.

We did it! Ralph completed his quest. I was really proud of him and his boat. I know he had to have tears in his eyes, but I couldn't look, for I didn't want him to see that mine were a little misty. (The older I get, the more emotional I'm becoming)

I was busy videotaping our entrance into the harbor. Looking a little to the left, over the bow and between a bunch of yachts we made out the Statue of Liberty. We were probably about a mile away, yet she stood out among the haze over the water. The New York leg took 53 hours, about seven hours ahead of schedule. Ralph's goal was to get a picture from inside his Intruder as we passed the statue. We idled around and were amazed how large she looked from our small boat about 50 yards away. I had forgotten about the size of the pedestal she stood on. There were two ferryboats docking with many of the tourist climbing in and out. Many were looking at us; we must have looked like some sort of refugees. We got a little video and a few pictures, before we decided to try to find our Uncle David who was to pick Ralph up and take him to the storage garage where Jim and Cheri left Ralph's car and trailer.

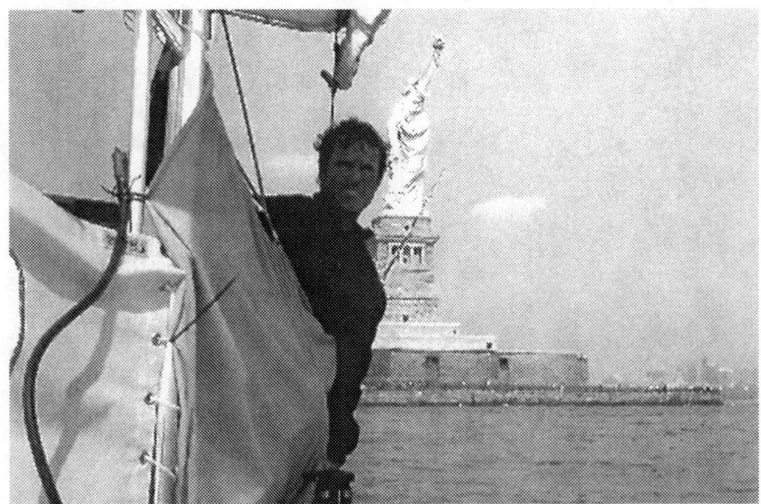

Bob leaning over to pose with the Statue of Liberty. Notice the breather (vent) for the 70 gallon fuel tank fastened to the T-top.

Ralph had to fly Jim and Cheri home after we were delayed in Bermuda. They left the car about 20 minutes away from Liberty State Park, where we had planned to dock, and pull out the boat. After spending about 10 minutes at the Statue of Liberty, we started looking for the Liberty Park Marina. We drove around the backside of the statue, almost completing our victory lap, and then preceded to head for the nearest shore. We decided to go to our left. There were several little dead ends and some fishermen on the rocks. I thought that Ralph should have driven a little further away from them in the event that they actually wanted to catch fish. Ralph was thinking again, and not paying attention to what was happening around him. He agreed and gave them a wider berth on our return, after finding a ramp without any signs, that couldn't be it.

The water was really nasty looking, besides from the greenish black with brown foam all along shore. There were pieces of trash everywhere; little pieces of wood floating among the Styrofoam bits and plastic. The smell was that of my kids' gym bags. I thought of the TV show Seinfeld, when Krammer was swimming laps in the bay. He slept on Elaine's bed and left it smelling so bad that she had to throw it away.

We did notice the white buoy marker that said no wake zone, and slowed down a little more, even though we were already going fairly slow. We kept going along the seawall, looking for anyone on shore that resembles our uncle. Not seeing him, we called him on our satellite phone, but he could hardly hear us, sometimes the reception was really terrible. Maybe it was because of the small metal bridge we were coming upon. Ralph was driving and hesitated before going underneath.

On the other side, we continued our search and I decided to try Uncle David again. I was starting to get mad at Ralph, for some reason he started driving faster and I couldn't hear my Uncle. I handed Ralph the phone, so that he would be forced to idle. All I could hear was that my uncle could now see us, and we weren't sure which way to steer. Just as Ralph idled down, we made out a police boat coming right for us with their blue lights flashing. Both of us instinctively looked all round and discovered that we were the only boat anywhere around. We thought that they must be customs; because we had called the number they gave us numerous times without any answer. We told Uncle David that we would call him back in a couple of minutes.

Receiving a ticket from the Port Authority officers for unknowingly venturing into the restricted area behind the Statue of Liberty even though the sign had been missing for months.

The lady in charge asked Ralph if we had just gone under that bridge, pointing behind us, since he was at the wheel. He said, "Yes sir." She corrected him with a "Mam!" I thought; this is going to be a great way to start off this conversation. She informed us, that we had just driven through a restricted zone. Ralph answered that we hadn't realized it, we hadn't seen any signs. She informed us, that there were marker buoys all around the backside of the Statue of Liberty. And besides, as captain of a boat, it was his responsibility to check out the local charts. She then asked him if he had any charts of this area. He replied, that he didn't see the need, since the website that he looked at of this area, said that Liberty Park Ramp was right next to the Statue of Liberty.

She asked us for our passports and registration. Ralph dug his out of the overhead compartment, while I went up to the bow to get mine out of the tied down cooler. By the time I made it back to the stern of our boat, the police boat had idled up to Ralph and the second officer received Ralph's papers over their bow, then started to back away. I held out my passport, for them to idle back and pickup. The second officer gave us a lecture on the proper procedure for transferring papers to an officer in another boat. We were supposed to gather all the papers then make the transfer at one time. We said yes sir, as they back away again. I muttered to Ralph, what did they think I was getting out of my backpack from my cooler? They had to be watching me?

Ralph started to inform them that we had just driven here from Bermuda and all we wanted to do was to find the ramp and meet up with our uncle to get this boat out of the water. This was the first time that any of them expressed any interest in the gas tanks that basically filled the interior of our Intruder. From their angle looking down, we must have looked like a floating bomb; they probably should have driven up with their guns drawn since we had just driven up to one of America's most famous monuments.

The lady commander went into their cockpit and started checking our papers. She started asking Ralph his address and stuff. He answered her and then added that all that information was on his passport. I told Ralph to just answer the questions. I didn't want any more trouble. The second officer seemed to lighten up a little and asked us some questions about our trip.

Ralph asked, "Are we were going to get a ticket?"

The officer said, "That it was up to his commander."

Ralph wanted to know more about the restricted zone buoys. The second officer said that the restricted buoys were spaced across the front of the Statue of Liberty entrance going all the way to the outside corner of shore. Ralph expressed his doubt that it was correctly marked. Ralph received his $75.00 ticket, and then Ralph told them that this should count as our government witness that proved that we had entered the Harbor. They told us that the ramp that we were looking for was at the other side, where we first looked. Ralph wanted to know if they could do our custom's check. They said that they could, but wouldn't because they were too busy, then drove off.

We talked about the fact that they were probably after us when we went under the bridge and we didn't even know it. We spotted our uncle after we called him on the phone again. He was talking to an officer in a squad car, about a hundred yards away. The officer drove to the point and put his red flashing lights on. Is this guy after us too? We weren't sure if we were allowed to bring the boat next to the seawall, but eventually he waved us over. He was really nice; he was going to escort my uncle over to the ramp and gave us more directions to the ramp.

As we drove around the front of the statue, we noticed that the white buoys indeed did say restricted, and we wondered if the corner one was also there, where we first drove around the corner. There wasn't anything anywhere near the corner where we entered the backside of the statue area. I told Ralph, that I didn't really pay any attention to the white buoys, because we were already idling, and I assumed they said no wake zone, like the one near the ramp. He said, that he didn't even notice them at all. He was too busy posing for pictures and taking pictures. If he had noticed them, he would have thought that they were also idle speed zone or something like that. If this is a restricted zone, they should have a lot more buoys, and maybe some official looking signs at the corners. We found out later, that there used to be a corner buoy, but it's been missing for months.

Just as we rounded the corner, two men on jet skis went right into the restricted zone doing all kinds of radical turns and spraying each other. I said, "I guess they'll be in trouble in a couple of minutes."

We drove slowly around the fishermen and they waved to us. It didn't look like we were going to have much of a fan fair. There were no newspaper or camera men anywhere in sight. The one officer with my uncle was at the ramp and soon another officer showed up. They both seemed really interested in the world record trip. Both of them were also at one time in the Coast Guard. They were able to validate our custom papers for us, and Ralph also had them sign a paper stated that we were indeed here in New York Harbor.

Ralph left with our uncle while, I started readying the boat for the trailer. I put all the wet stuff in separate bags for each of us; stowing all the gear in hatches, taking down the wind block on the side of the cockpit, and repacking all the electronics, removing as much loose stuff as possible.

I watch the two jet skiers go by and start to load their skis onto their trailers. Nobody seemed to question them, and they soon drove away. I guess the restricted zone was only for tourist.

After a while, one of the officers came back with a camera and took some pictures of the Intruder and me. He was going to a donut shop and asked if I wanted some coffee or something. I said that I would love a soda. He said he would be right back. It took him a while; he had a call while coming back, and wouldn't let me give him any money for the Pepsi. (See, a lot of the people in New York are really nice.)

He asked, "How much fuel did you use coming from Bermuda?"

"300 gallons, about 35 to spare." I answered.

"How much further could you go on 35 gallons?"

"Now that the boat is light again, probably all day, maybe seven to ten hours at 25 miles per hour, maybe more."

Chapter 11
New York to Florida

We loaded the boat on the trailer and talked in the parking lot for quite a while. Realizing that we never called Harbour Radio of Bermuda since we actually were on shore, we called them. They again congratulated us. I thought they had a good time tracking us. It was probably something they looked forward to when they came to work each day. We wondered if they had taken bets whether we'd make it or not, and also if they had predicted our time of arrival.

We turned down my uncle's offer to go to Long Island and spend the night. We would have really wanted to, but this was Friday night and both wanted to be home for mother's day on Sunday. We tried to take our uncle out to dinner, I was still thinking of my stake dinner. He said that he had already eaten and thought that he should start going back home. It was almost a three hour drive back to his house in Long Island, in the traffic. I was a little depressed; I really wanted to take him to a stake house. We took the last couple of pictures and said goodbye.

Bob, Uncle David and Ralph at Liberty State Park boat ramp. Uncle David came by to help Ralph pick up his car and trailer from the storage building twenty minutes away. He also helped with some of the photos.

Ralph started driving and it wasn't long before he wanted me to take over. We were both hungry and decided to stop at a Boston Market for dinner. It wasn't a stake house but that was ok, it wouldn't be the same without my Uncle. Before leaving the parking lot, one of us suggested that we take a short nap in the car before heading back on the highway. The next thing we knew, 8 hours had passed. We were probably both lucky we stopped for a quick nap. Driving home was probably the most dangerous part of our trip.

Before getting back on the highway, we stopped to get some window paint and made signs about our trip. We also hung our flags that made the whole 1500 miles in the North Atlantic, in the rod holders on top of the T-top. The heavy canvas one with the Dreamboat logo, snapped off before we even got on the interstate. Ralph drove back a mile to retrieve it. We tied a rope around it, and added three more plastic wire ties. A hundred miles down the road; we found out that we were only sporting the plastic pipe that the flag was attached to. Someone was going to have a nice souvenir of our trip.

We talked about what we would do differently, if we were making the same trip again? All the electronics would be hard wired in with a waterproof plug on the inside of the cabinet. We'd bring better wet suits and a survivor sleeping bag. One of the most important things for driving at night in the cold would be a really good mug warmer, one that would really heat up soup and coffee, but not spill in high seas. Charts and know the course in advance. Snorkel gear for diving once we arrived in Bermuda. Waterproof bags made for the cameras so the cameras could be more accessible.

After we had gone through a few states, we started using up the extra 35 gallons of gas from the jury jugs stored in the boat. Later, we decided to try out our lighter plug crock-pot with the rusty soup cans without labels left over from our trip. After we poured the soup cans, we decided to finish the videotape with a bad reenactment of us preparing our soup, which tasted really good when we ate it thirty minutes later in a gas station parking lot, sitting on the ground.

While talking to Jill, I found out that her brother borrowed our van, when his car broke down while he was in Merritt Island. Since he lived in Orlando, I would be able to pick it up and save Ralph a couple of hours. He wouldn't have to drop me off. I arrived home at 4:30 on Sunday morning, May 13, 2007 after being gone for a total of 18 partial days.

Newspaper Article

From: The Royal Gazette by Sam Strangeways

(published May 14, 2007)

Made it! Brothers back home as tiny boat defies 6ft waves

Two brothers who set out in a tiny open fishing boat from the States to Bermuda to prove it could withstand high seas have made it safely home.

Ralph and Bob Brown arrived in New York Harbour on Friday afternoon after leaving St. George's on Wednesday in their 21 ft motor boat.

The pair had spent more than a week on the Island waiting for the right weather conditions after arriving here from North Carolina on May 2.

They believe they set a new world record for the longest unescorted oceanic crossing in a shallow vessel known as a flats boat on the 675 mile journey over. If so, they broke it on the 775 mile trip back to the US.

Father-of-three Ralph, 48, who designed and built the Intruder 1, spoke to The Royal Gazette—by telephone last night after driving home to Florida.

He said the boat encountered four to six foot high waves on the journey home across the Atlantic. "We thought we were going into five or nine foot seas but they were much smaller than that. We had no weather problems whatsoever other than it got very, very, very cold.

Mr. Brown said the voyage was never about setting a world record but rather proving the model of boat he designed—which his company Dram Boats sells for between $20,000 and $35,000—could handle six to eight foot seas.

"It handled flawlessly," he said. "The boat did everything we thought it would do. We ran into six to eight foot seas without any problem. We wanted nothing bigger than 12 foot but we didn't get near that." The pair were warned against the trip by both the US Coast Guard and Bermuda Maritime Operations Centre but Mr. Brown said he believed in the boat so didn't feel there was a risk. “We kept in contact with Bermuda Harbour Radio the entire way,” he said, adding that he and his brother did a victory lap in the boat around the Statue of Liberty on Friday.

“It was great. My daughter, who's 11, was hanging onto me big time today. My son wished he could have done it.”

He paid tribute to the Bermudians he met while on the Island. “I have never been anywhere where I felt like the people were nicer,” he said. “They just bend over backwards to try to help you.”

To read more about the trip visit dreamboats.net.

Newspaper Article

From: The Royal Gazette (in Bermuda) by Tim Smith (published May 30, 2007)

‘Suicide’ boaters fined for Liberty victory lap

After earning a reputation as two of the craziest men to cross the Atlantic in recent memory, Ralph and Bob Brown decided to mark the completion of their record-breaking voyage in typically flamboyant style.

But the brothers' victory celebration—a lap of honour around the Statue of Liberty—landed them in hot water when eagle-eyed officials promptly hit them with a $75 ticket for breaking strict security regulations.

Now the American pair have been bailed out by a Royal Gazette reader who was so impressed by their Ultimate Bermuda Suicide Challenge he decided to pay their fine himself.

They embarked on the North Carolina to New York via Bermuda unescorted mission as a publicity stunt to prove a 21-foot flats boat, which is normally designed for shallow water fishing, was capable of handling the ocean. Peter Michelson, a Bermudian living in New York, had followed the Brown brothers' antics via this newspaper website.

When he spotted on their blog shortly afterwards that they had been fined for the Statue of Liberty incident, Mr. Michelson stepped in. "I read that they had received the ticket for going around the Statue of Liberty and thought that wasn't the kind of welcome they needed after their accomplishment. They went through all that, and got a $75 ticket," he said.

"So I emailed them and told them I was a Bermudian who wanted to pay their ticket, and I put a cheque in the post for them. I told them to pay the ticket and then reimburse themselves with my cheque."

The area surrounding the statue became out of bounds when security was stepped up in the wake of September 11. Ralph and Bob say they had no idea they were breaking the law.

Ralph said: " I did a victory lap around the Statue of Liberty. I guess you can't do that. They called it a restricted zone violation. The sign was down where we entered the zone. They said it was my fault, I should have had a chart. Welcome home."

A message from Ralph on his website explains how the pair got fined: "Three nice port authority officers showed up in a Police cruiser and wrote us a $75 ticket, about 20 to 30 minutes after we got there.

"It was nice of them to provide the Government documentation of our arrival for the world record certification. In Bermuda, people asked us to sign a copy of the newspaper with our pictures on it. In NY Harbour, we got to sign a summons. See how much we are alike."

After arriving in Bermuda at the half-way point of their trip, Floridians Ralph and Bob were urged to abandon their voyage on safety grounds by Bermuda Maritime Operations Centre and US Coast Guard officials.

However, they decided to press ahead regardless, and completed the second leg of the journey in about two days.

On this point, Ralph added: "You know at first I thought the people from Harbour Radio were giving me a hard time. You know, they turned out to be like the rest of Bermuda, some of the nicest guys in the world.

"I felt like I made so many friends in your country. You know I will be back and I will tell all my friends about your country." About the donation, Ralph added: "You know, you guys from Bermuda are the nicest people I have ever met. Several people have stayed in touch with us by email. The kindness has not stopped since I left. It is unbelievable."

Chapter 12
The Saga Continues

From the e-mails that I have received from Ralph, he's been working on overload. He's been sending out thank you notes to everyone. Trying to up-date his website: dreamboats.net, visit with his family, clean up the borrowed Intruder and put it back the way it was before he equipped it with the extra fuel tanks, etc.; make a few interviews for the radio magazines and radio talk shows; talk to all the people interested in his trip including quite a few investors. He's had a lot of people interested in purchasing a boat, but since he doesn't have any completed to sell, and doesn't built any without a large down payment at this time, they aren't in production at this time. He's expecting to start up soon.

Ralph had used my cell phone on the way home from New York and somehow a magazine editor got hold of it. I spent an hour giving him an interview of the trip. I thought that was kind of cool. Eventually Ralph also was interviewed and Ralph sent him a CD with all our pictures and the short version of my journal that I wrote on the way back to Florida. The editor told me that a lot of crackpots say they are going to do the Bermuda Challenge in small boats. Ralph had mailed him a letter telling him of his intentions of taking his 21-footer to Bermuda. The editor put Ralph's letter with all the other crackpots. He said that he was really glad that we actually did the trip, he said, "GOOD JOB!"

Almost everyday his website changed. I noticed that he's almost completely eliminated the word "suicide". He's been getting a lot of flack about it. And of course, it was never anything about suicide. He finally put a picture of the location of Bermuda on his site. I've been trying to get him to do that since we returned. I found that I wasn't the only one who didn't know where it was. Most people think it is somewhere near the Bahamas, less than a hundred miles from Florida. And the ones that know it's off the coast of North Carolina; think it's less than 300 miles, like I did.

Cleaning out the van, I came across my straw hat that I had for over a year and was my savior from the sun on the trip. Well, it shrunk so much after it dried out that it no longer fit on my head. It was a sad moment when I tossed it into the trash can. It was just about worn out anyway. I had reglued the weaving several times with you guess it, E-6000 the glue we used several times on the trip.

I've been making copies of the videos from the mounted cameras that we thought were ruined. They were submerged in salt water when the wave broke over the bow while Ralph was up front with his dry storage cooler opened. I had been letting the tapes dry out for about a week now. I wasn't sure if I wanted to waste my VCR putting in tapes that were covered in salt water. Then one of my painting customers gave me an old VCR that she was going to throw away. After unsticking the tape from the plastic housing, the tapes were surprisingly good. Almost all the video was clear, but in reality very boring to watch.

One of the cameras was mounted on the T-top facing forward and the other facing aft. You could see about three-foot of the bow and the water out in front. The waves were still relatively small because this was the footage of the beginning of the trip leaving North Carolina. Some of the tapes had really interesting stuff, if it were edited down to maybe a 30-minute tape. Both cameras were running at the same time and only lasted for the first 12 hours of the trip, including a couple of hours on land before we launched. We were lucky that Ralph didn't reinsert the tape that he didn't think recorded anything. We had forgotten that some of the VCR's automatically rewind the tapes. The batteries died before we reached the bigger stuff out in the Atlantic, despite several attempts to recharge them.

I've been working on this journal in most of my free time. I want to get it all down on paper before I forget anything. I'm not planning on doing a repeat trip anytime soon, but I have to admit, I'm already missing it. Only the next time, I'd like to do it with everyone's blessings and tons of dive equipment so I could get to see a little of what's underwater. Everything was so beautiful there and we didn't get to really enjoy any of it, except the town of St George and some of Hamilton.

Ralph called me a couple of days ago and asked me it I could come over on the 24th of May. He was to be interviewed for a TV news station. Something about a follow-up from a story they did several years ago. I first told him, that I was probably too busy, but in the end, I decided to take my motorcycle, a 1980 Honda 900. The bike is teal green with a little surface rust, but generally looks pretty good for its age. It burns oil and doesn't have a working speedometer.

After topping off the oil, 1½ quarts, I put on my gray motorcycle jacket and took off with my red backpack bungeed on the sissy bar. I brought with me, all my paper work from my trip, I was hoping we'd spend some time reviewing my notes for errors. Using my map from Map Quest, I arrived in Hudson, Florida in just short of three hours. I called Ralph for a landmark to locate his street, without a speedometer, map quest just gets you in the ball park without the actual maps. My printer was out of colored ink, and the maps don't print without ink.

Driving down the dirt road, I drove through the gate into a chained linked work site with several mobile offices with the lean-to awnings. There were several metal buildings all around with molds and boat projects in various stages of completion. Marino was in one of the buildings grinding some fiberglass on his own personal project. Shadow the guard dog walked up to the front of my bike and dropped his nasty orange ball on the ground. It was covered in white dust. Ralph was talking on a cell phone and washing one of his customer's boats. I helped him finish, since this was one of the boats that he was taking down to the boat ramp as part of the interview.

Ralph had called several of his customers and asked them if they were available to meet him with their boats at the ramp. The news people wanted to interview them about their boats. Ralph managed to get three of the 18-foot Intruders, the family that lent him the 21-foot Intruder and their boat, and the guy that bought the first 23-foot Dreamsurfer ever sold.

Close to 2:30 the cameraman and the lady interviewer showed up and spent about two and half-hours interviewing everyone. She then had us put the Intruders in the water and went for a ride. She drove part of the way, while talking into the camera. They also took a lot of footage of the other Intruders driving by us. Everything went well, but Ralph though they were doing more of story about the boats, a follow-up to the story they did on Ralph about 5 years ago, not so much about the Bermuda trip.

Going back to his boat yard, I found out some information about the trip I wasn't aware of. First of all, the coordinates Ralph had for Bermuda was 15 miles off the southwest corner. That is why the Harbour Radio gave us the first set of coordinates on the Northwest corner. Had we gone to that spot, we would have been north of the reefs that they wanted us to avoid and we would have had a relatively straight shot into the Cut, thus, eliminating the long drive around the southeast part of the island. This whole thing would have been avoided if I had let Ralph change the mounted GPS with the first set of numbers from Harbour Radio. I was under the assumption that we would see land from Ralph's first set of numbers. This is how I found out that Bermuda is really a circle with the northwest part of the circle underwater, thus the underwater reefs ten miles off shore. I discovered another name for Bermuda, probably because of all the underwater obstructions. Bermuda's 138 islands were sometimes called the Isle of Devils, littered with many ship wrecks. (not a term used very often today.)

We spent most of our time the circle area of the map of Bermuda. That area is Saint Georges Parrish, and I have to say the whole island was inhabited by the nicest group of people I ever came across. Strangers held doors open; it was easy to start up conversations on the buses or in lines at the grocery store. Everyone use the words "please" and "thank you" everywhere we went on the island. Our only bad experience was when we were both over tired on our entrance into the island. If I had let Ralph plug in the coordinates into the main GPS and drive to those coordinates I'm sure that would have been a great experience also. We would have arrived an hour or two earlier and Anne and Phillip would have been there to greet us as planned.

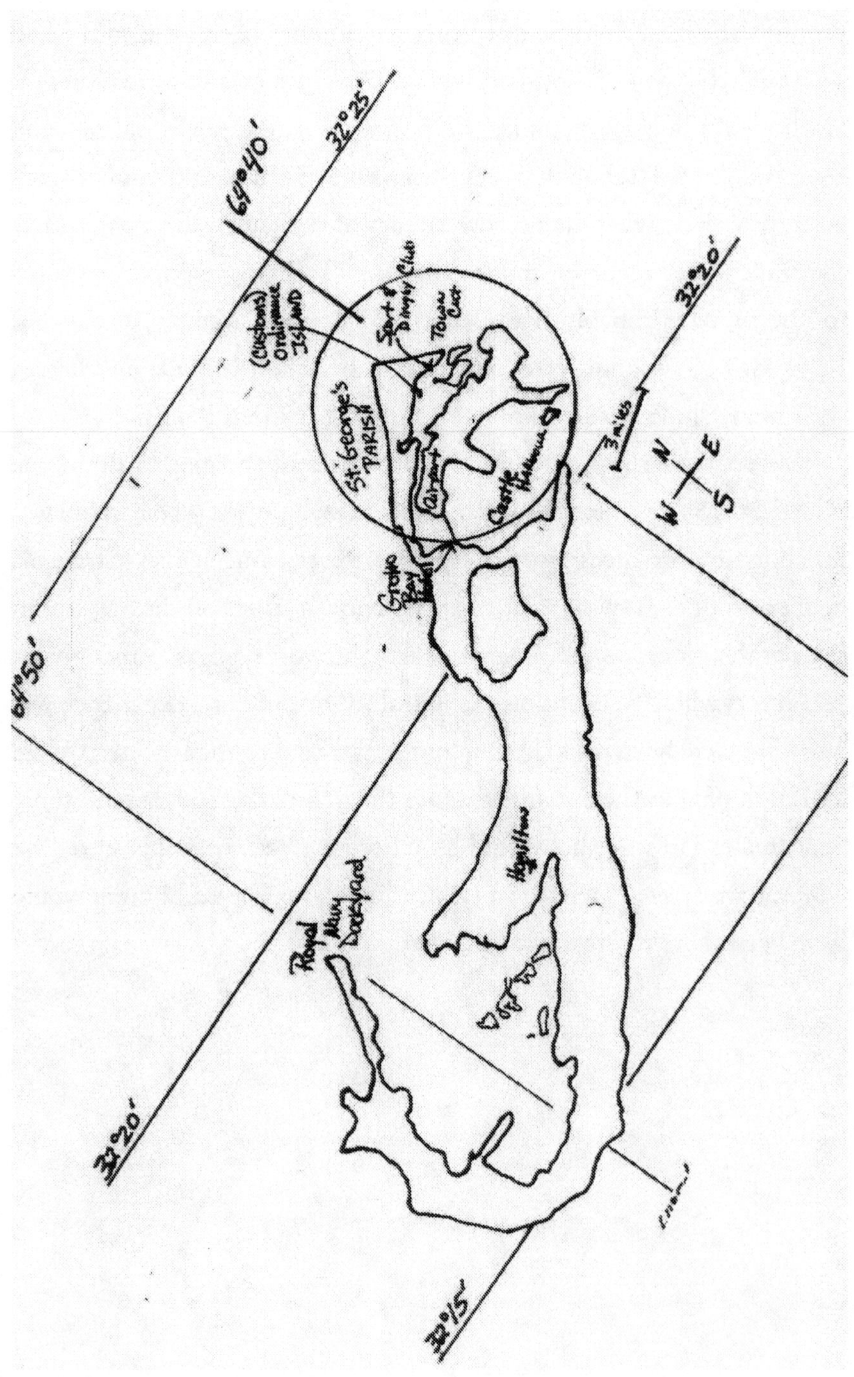

64°40'
32°25'
32°20'
(Customs)
Ordinance
Island
Sport &
Dinghy Club
Town Cut
St. George's
PARISH
Airport
Castle
Harbour
3 miles
N
E
W
S
64°50'
Hamilton
Royal
Navy
Dockyard
32°20'
32°15'

I left Ralph in Hudson after we developed the last of the film from my surf camera at the one-hour developing. We were looking forward to some of the pictures of the salty Suzuki. It didn't do reality justice. The whole motor was almost solid white with salt, it didn't show that. An hour into my return ride home, I had to stop and fuel up my motorcycle and wash off the love bugs from my helmet shield. I drove though about a half-hour of pouring rain near the halfway point going home. I turned into my driveway just before 10:00.

The next week or so, I worked on my journal, now thinking more about publishing it. I called the local newspapers and never received a call back. I guess maybe there really isn't enough interest in this story to warrant any local press.

Finally after e-mailing a local writer for the Hometown News, who was just finishing a story about a long distance surfboard paddler. Who paddled from Miami to Jacksonville and set a world record for the longest distance paddled. I received a call on my cell phone. The writer wanted to know more about our trip. By June 2nd, I was able to e-mail him and report to him that it was official. According to The World Record Academy: Ralph and Bob Brown are the holders of the longest unescorted oceanic crossing of a flats boat. The Record Academy had just sent out a press release about our trip.

I finally finished my photo album and labeled all the pictures. Many of my friends said I should print the story and include as many pictures as I can. I have a friend of mine who is a journalist living in Brazil; checking with his friend living in Hawaii on the contract I sent him from a publishing company. Hopefully if everything is affordable, I'll be able to wrap this story up and go on to finishing my fiction book I've been writing for almost a year now. The story is about 4 high-school kids, who are athletes and surfers. I'm not sure of the title yet, but I'm on page 210 now and plan to finish with a little over 300 total pages.

From some New York e-mails, we found out that the Verranzano Narrows Bridge between Staten Island and Brooklyn was the bridge we went under entering the New York Harbor. The Brooklyn Bridge was further up the Harbor, past the Statue of Liberty.

The Florida Today printed an article in the section for the local news called 'The Press' for Merritt Island, Cocoa Beach, and Cape Canaveral on June 20th, 2007 entitled "Brothers set boating record". They had two big colored pictures. Several friends that hadn't known about the trip congratulated me upon reading it. When I tried to tell them that it really wasn't that big of a deal, they said that they would never, never ever attempt it.

On Wednesday, July 18th, Guinness Book of World Records™ sent Ralph e-mail stating that they authorized the new category: The Longest Nonstop Oceanic Voyage in a Flats Boat.

While Ralph was trying to locate paper work for the record books, he came across the weather charts from the first two days of our first crossing on the way to Bermuda. We had estimated the wave heights up to about 8 foot on our second day at sea. The NWS/NCEP-Ocean Prediction Center recorded the Average height of the highest one third of the waves by buoys to be in the three meter range or nine and a half foot range. I guess I'm one of those surfers who don't like to over estimate the size of the waves.

While e-mailing several of the people that gave me business cards in Bermuda, I've been trying to put a face to all the cards that I collected. I emailed Sean who works with Container Ship Management, thinking that he might be in several pictures that I had from the Friday night at the Dinghy and Sports Club. He wasn't the person, who I thought he was, but he sent me picture of himself and I remembered briefly talking to him. Sean was able to identify several people that I didn't have emails for.

Sean informed me that this was a small world. His cousin Terry from North Carolina, also a Bermudian, was the lady that we bought our gas from the morning that we left on our trip across the Atlantic. She evidently thought that we were joking, until several Coast Guard personal came by the station asking questions. She called her mother in Bermuda to see if she knew anything about us. Terry's mother called Sean, because he moved in maritime circles and he told her that he had met us after happy hour at the Dinghy club.

On November 5th, 2007 Ralph received a phone call from Guinness Book of World Records™ that we had been awarded the record.

The current record for "Longest non-stop ocean voyage in a flats boat" is: The longest non-stop ocean voyage in a flats boat was 1245.63 km (774 miles) was set by Ralph and Robert Brown (USA) who traveled from St. Georges, Bermuda to New York Harbor, USA, from 9-11 May 2007.

Ralph's Press Release:

November 7, 2007

Guinness Book of World Records™ has certified the "Longest Non-Stop Ocean Voyage in a Flats Boat," Record holders to be Ralph and Robert Brown of Tampa May and Merritt Island, Florida. The 774 mile voyage from St. Georges Bermuda to New York Harbor (May 9-May 11, 2007) was the final leg of a 1547 mile voyage from Atlantic Beach N.C. to Bermuda to New York Harbor that the made in a 21-ft. flats boat without a cabin or a keel.

Ralph Brown made the trip to prove his flats boat design could take heavy seas. Bob (Robert) made the trip because he is a great brother and the previous first mate bailed out at the last minute. The 21 ft. flats boat was an Intruder 21 produced by Dream Boats, Inc. of Hudson Florida.

The brothers were at sea for 5 days in the North Atlantic and had to endure waves up to 9 feet and winds in excess of 30 mph.

Ralph Brown
352-346-2365
Dream Boat, Inc.
8424 Arcola Ave.
Hudson, Florida 34667

Chapter 13
Quotes from Ralph Brown "dreamboats.net"

DREAMSURFER 230
(Ralph's first boat design)

"About five years ago I began an earnest approach to boat building centered around the concept of building a boat that can cruise in the shallow waters of Florida's Gulf coastal area, as well as handle the rough blue water seas to reach the middle gulf fishing grounds. The Dreamsurfer 230 is the culmination of our efforts, achieving a draft at idle speed of 10-12 inches and a cruising draft of 6-8 inches. **THIS IS THE ENTIRE DRAFT!** Our Patent Pending Propulsion unit encompasses a recessed propeller system and unique hull design that protects the prop from damage. No trim tabs are required with the Dreamsurfer 230."

Ralph Brown, President

The Dreamsurfer rides on top of the water instead of down in it, and the propeller is protected, limiting damage potential. Also, the boat is significantly less likely to hurt a manatee than most boats. It is also much less likely to hurt a human being.

- Large Walk-in Restroom ; Bait Well; Under Seat Cooler; Freshwater shower; Anchor Locker; Two Built-in Tackle Boxes; Docking (Head) Lights; Raw Water wash down; Port a Potty; Four fishing Rod Holders; VHF Radio; Fresh water shower and sink; Hummingbird Fish Finder; 3 year Engine Warranty; 7 year Hull Warranty;
- Three basic set-up options: Fishing seats; "U" shaped bench seats; or extra large cooler

C-18 INTRUDER
(the smaller version of the one we took to Bermuda)

"Floats in 5-8 inches depending on engine size and passenger load. With a jack plate, it runs is less. Just like you dreamed, super stable, super dry and super smooth. Run all weekend on one tank of gas. (Results may vary depending upon actual usage, and size of engine.)

Boat, motor, and trailer package Includes: 100% fiberglass composite hull; console; no-feed back steering; 18 gallon fuel tank; 100% sealed and filled safety hull; Ace Steering wheel; five cleats; skis storage compartments with hatches; three eye bolts; self bailing deck with ball valve scuppers; four inch rigging tube; front rigging tube for trolling motor; rub rail; tinted acrylic wind shield; Yamaha pre-rig, with tach, water pressure, gas, oil, and speed gages; Igloo Cooler with seat cushion, aluminum four blade prop; and a seven year hull warranty."

INTRUDER 21
(the one we took to Bermuda)

The Intruder 21 floats in 7-8 inches, gets up in 10-12 inches, and runs in less than 4 inches. The ride is incredible with smoothness and dryness. Comes standard with eight storage bins of which six are convertible to live wells, seven fool three storage locker for rods and skies, even though it is rated for 150 hp, it will run quite well with a 90 hp. 100% of all test rides given to date say it is one of the best riding boats they have ever been on. The price is an introductory price and extremely competitive.

Messages taken off Ralph's web-site dreamboats.net

Why did we go to Bermuda? **It was supposed to be about the boat. It turned into; about the two nuts who had the guts to do it.**

The purpose of the trip was to show that our 21 Ft. Intruder could handle 6-8 Ft waves. Lots of boats can handle 6-8 Ft. waves but can they also run in less than six inches, not beat in a chop, and still be reasonably dry. I told a lot of people it could run in 6 ft seas, most did not believe me. I guess one too many laughed at what I said. So I decided to make a statement.

I could not think of anything better than a trip to Bermuda, then on to New York Harbor. It was never about the record, until I learned it would probably be a record. You can thank Bob Hite, NBC Channel 8 Anchor for that, as he was the first to point it out.

The trip had to unescorted to show that we did trust in the seaworthiness of the boat, and of course God smiling on us, not a larger boat following us.

(There is a picture on his web-site showing a yellow 18 foot Intruder with 5 people on one side of Eric Marshall's boat. Very stable, several with their hands in the hip pockets.)

(A second picture with two guys shark fishing 5 miles off Crystal River, Fla. In another 18 ft Intruder, belonging to Mike Embach.)

Details pulled directly off Ralph's website (BLOGS)

Monday, April 30, 2007
Bermuda Trip Begins

The two Brown brothers began their first leg of the perilous journey to Bermuda and back to New York Harbor, 1400 miles of open ocean. Bob Brown is accompanying his brother Ralph Brown… At 6:00 am Monday morning, the continued preparation began. At around 7:00 am, Ralph and Bob went to fill up four gas tanks totaling nearly 300 gallons of gas. That's 2000 pounds of fuel. An hour and a half later they were at the dock and ready to go. After meeting with the Mayor of Atlantic Beach and making some final arrangements, the Intruder 21 was in the water and all systems were go. A chase boat followed Ralph and Bob out for almost 10 miles, to allow for some photographs and media video. And then just like that, they were off in the horizon. We later received our first satellite phone call from Ralph with a report that everything was going as planned. Due to the extreme weight of the fuel, they were traveling at a slower speed then originally intended. Ralph hopes this will change when they burn off some fuel. More updates to come when we next hear from Ralph. Leave Ralph a comment to encourage him on his journey.

Nick dill said…

Good Luck with your Journey! You will be there soon enough. History in the making! Boat On! Nick May 1, 12:32 pm

Thursday, May 3, 2007 by Ralph Brown
Bermuda at Grotto Bay

We arrived in Bermuda on Wednesday at about 1:00 pm, There was no small commotion. No one could believe that we had made the crossing in a 21 ft, flats boat. Everyone seemed to believe it was the first time anyone had ever done that. We got to meet a bunch of government officials. They turned out to be very helpful.

The crossing actually went quite well taking 51 hours including a lot of down time on the phone. My Brother Bob, who had never been on the boat until we started for Bermuda, was surprised the first time we went over some six footers. He then realized why I was so confident in the boat. That turkey, later told me that he thought I would turn back at the first big waves. The boat handled the waves beautifully. Most of the waves were 3-5 ft in size with occasional larger ones, even up to eight foot. We only had five waves come over the bow and only two as far as the windshield. Unfortunately the wind was up most of the way 10 – 25 mph and blew a lot of water back on us.

It looks like there is a front coming through from N.Y. and we will have to wait here for a day or two to sit out the weather, life is rough, stuck in Bermuda, but somebody has to do it. I want to remind everyone that I am the builder, and this is not something I would recommend to do at home. If you are ever in Bermuda stop in at Triangle Dive Shop and Blue Hole Water Sports.

www.trianglediving.com and www.blueholewater.bm

Friday, May 4, 2007 by Ralph Brown Heading for NY

We have been here in Bermuda for two days waiting out the front. It appears that we will be able to leave today, Friday, May 4, late afternoon. We added a new wave brake to the front of our console in case we have to go through waves bigger than 10 ft. We have already been through a few 8 ft waves. The wave brake is absolutely perfect in what we wanted. The wonderful folks at Ocean Sales St. Georges Bermuda built it for us. They did an excellent job on short notice. www.oceansails.com If you are ever in Bermuda see Steve, Suzanne, and Rod. The stay has been fun. The people, excellent and very helpful. Everything here is a little expensive. Our Suzuki 115 four stroke has run great.

We have also met two different people in Bermuda who have expressed an interest in investing in Dream Boats, and two separate individuals who have expressed an interest in opening up dealerships in Bermuda, and one in N.C. Details will have to be worked out.

The people at Bermuda, Radio have agreed to track us back to N.Y. on radar. We will be reporting to them Six hours. The Royal Gazette has updated articles if you want to read them.

Anonymous said…

Dad, I just hop u know that mom is really mad, and the sooner that you get home the better… May 9, 2007 6:45pm

Anonymous said….

Deep water in the ocean, just wait till you get back! No Coast Guard approval? What the heck! Incredibly stupid and selfish!

Notombstone said….

Yes, it is selfish for someone to take chances to make it in this world. You can talk about the boat till your blue in the face. But they aren't going to believe you till you prove it. At a glance the flats all look similar. Doing this is going to get everyone's attention, maybe when you say something, now they will listen. May 13, 2007 3:59 pm

Saturday, May 5, 2007 by Ralph Brown
Still in Bermuda

Last night we were supposed to leave, pending one last weather report. It showed 18 ft waves 100 miles off of N.Y. That means they would have been 20 – 30 ft in the Gulf Stream. While Bob and I might be a little gutsy, we are not crazy. It looks like we are going to have to wait until Tuesday night or Wednesday morning to leave. That should put us in at about noon Friday, in New York Harbor.

While the people in Bermuda have treated us like royalty, we were even given honorary membership in the St. George's Boat and Dinghy Club; this trip would not be possible without the four greatest people in my life: Anne, my wife, Phillip, Heath, and Brittany, my children. Anne has gone way beyond any expectations to help me. She even volunteered to accompany me across the Atlantic when my first mate, had to back out due to unforeseen circumstances. That is a pretty brave woman.

As far as we can tell no one has ever made the crossing in a single engine flats boat before. Most of the men, we met in Bermuda says they would not do it. (They have more common sense than I.) Most of them have been across in much larger boats. All kinds of Government officials, even the American Consulate have been trying to talk us out of going on to N.Y. Even the newspaper reported that the Bermuda Radio strongly recommends we abandon the rest of the trip. Some even called Bob and I crazy idiots, I still call it proof. After they realized we were not going to be persuaded to cancel they became very helpful in planning the rest of the trip.

I know in the beginning she was rightfully skeptical as any responsible woman would be when her crazy husband took much needed money and started a boat company. She has put up with me for five years while we struggled to get this started.

Lord willing we shall arrive in N.Y. Harbor on Friday.

Tom said…
…well, I think we have to keep our champagne bottles at freezer few more days. Good luck, Guys! Tom May 5, 2007 12:17 pm
http://www.worldrecordsacademy.org

anonymous said…

Morons!! May 9, 2007 12:22 pm

Monday, May 7, 2997 by Ralph Brown
Waiting on the Perfect Storm

From North Carolina to Bermuda, (675 miles of open ocean), From Bermuda to New York Harbor, (775 miles of open ocean) in an UNESCORTED FLATS BOAT. By definition a flats boat is a single engine, low profile, open fishing style boat, that can run in less than one foot of water. This Intruder 21 can run in 4 – 6 inches of water.

Currently there is a major storm off the coast of N. C. and another forming near N.Y. some people have called them the perfect storm. We are waiting out this situation. I flew back to Florida to take care of some business issues while Bob stayed with the boat, to make some preparations. My temporary cell phone number is 352-346-2365.

I will be flying back to Bermuda on Tuesday, May 8 and planning to slip out the back behind the storm either late Tuesday or early Wednesday to be in New York Harbor about noon Friday.

Wednesday, May 9, 2007 by Ralph Brown
On Their Way to New York

I received 2 satellite phone calls from Ralph today (Tuesday May 9th). They seemed to be doing very well. They were both very excited, and looking forward to the venture. Ralph said that they were expecting 5-9 footers today with 2-5 footers the rest of the trip, hopefully. They were approximately 70 miles off the coast of Bermuda when the engine oil light came on. They immediately turned the engine off, dropped in their sea anchors, called a boat mechanic, and did some investigating. Ralph said that they now have a tether system (which you can see in the pics) that they devised, so they tied themselves to the boat before leaning over to check out the engine. Come to find out the light came on to notify them to do an oil change, which they had just performed before the left. They were told by the mechanic that there was no problem, so they fired it up and kept on going. Some of the pics show some of Ralph and Bob's new friends that they met in Bermuda. Their friends have really helped them out a lot, from building a wave brake, and giving advice, to charting their every move by radar. Stay posted right here for the latest up to date info on the trip. I'll be sure to let you know what's happening when I hear from Ralph and Bob next.

Anonymous said…
Crazy……   May 10, 2007 1:31 pm

Anonymous said….

How about an update?? Are they safe? In NYC? Back to Bermuda? Awaiting rescue? May 11, 2007 6:37 am

Mark said…..
Who cares??? They are a pair of idiots! May 11, 2007 8:07 am

Friday, May 11, 2007
Almost There!

Ralph called just a few minutes ago stating they were 112 miles from New York Harbor and that they will be glad to get their feet on dry land. I know that their family's' will be glad to have them home & and sound.

It has been a long journey and they have accomplished their goal. To prove that the intruder is a sea-worthy flats boat. A boat that can go in shallow water anywhere from six inches of water and also be sea-worthy for those short trips several miles out.

They stated that the weather was not bad at all and the seas were somewhat calm. They apologize to anyone that may have thought their trip was unsafe. They always felt that their safety was important that is why they watched the weather report and waited a week to come home. They also had brought aboard a satellite phone, an Emergency Position Indicating Radio beacon (EPIRB), and they wore a tether that was tied on the boat at times. They both are very good in the water having grown up surfing in Cocoa Beach.

Thank God they are almost there.

Anonymous said...
Good to hear they will make it.... Bravo
May 11. 2007 2:57 pm

Anonymous said...
*Any updates??? Did they make it to **New York**??*
May 11, 2007 4:23 pm

Anonymous said...
RALPH I CAN'T BELIEVE YOU MADE IT. I GUESS ALL OUR PRAYERS WERE ANSWERED. ANNE MUST BE SO HAPPY YOUR SAFE. COME BACK TO FLORIDA SOON. May 11, 2007 5:19 pm

Friday, May 11, 2007
They Made It!

Well, they made it! Ralph called today at 2:00pm to say that in the distance they could see New Jersey, and they were soon to be pulling into the bay. He said the trip went pretty well. Thankful, the seas remained relatively calm. They expected 5-9 footers for a short time; however they were 2-6 most of the way home. He said, "we made it, we traveled over 1500 miles of open waters and we did it all in an Intruder flats boat." For those who say that the Intruder 21 is not a sea worthy boat, think again. It seems that Ralph has just proved that it is. We'll have more details (and I'm sure pictures) to share soon, probably from Ralph himself. Can you imagine the scene now, a yellow 21 foot flats boat pulling into New York harbor after a 1500 mile journey? I'm sure we all would have loved to have seen that. Way to go Ralph and Bob, you did it!

Anonymous said...
Hooray!!!! Great job. May 11, 2007 11:37 pm

Tom said...
Congratulations!...for now [...]
Tom World Records Academy www.worldrecordsacademy.org
Notice: "don't try this at home"; for future Record breakers: if you don't have the Coast Guard approval, you will not get yours record recognized!
May 12, 2007 4:02 am

Anonymous said...
Congratulations guys. Obviously the boat works, and you guys did too! All the best, Geoff PS thanks for the call
May 12, 2007 7:41 am

Lady Sasha said….

Impressive! *This shows the American Entrepreneur is still a strong force to be reckoned with… Believing in your dreams… and making it happen! Congratulations! And for all those who believe….* ***It's possible!*** *Lady Sasha May 12, 2007 10:57 am*

Friend said…

Ralph and Bob CONGRADULATIONS!!!! Hats off to both of you, I can't wait to hear it all first hand. Record or no record the bottom line is a great quality boat through low waters, high waves and unsinkable, you can't beat that.. Great job Ralph… See you when you get back!!!! May 12, 2007 12:31 pm

Sunday, May 13, 2007
Home at Last

I just got home a few minutes ago, it is 4:30 am. I am so excited. It is Sunday Morning, and I have been driving all night, I will be in church today. Check it out, Northcliffe Baptist Church in Spring Hill, Fl. For all you people who have focused on the danger, I understand your concerns, but also let me encourage you to think about your heritage, The Great American Spirit. The Great American Spirit, with God given guidance made this the greatest country in the history of the world. Our fore fathers endured great hardship and great risk to provide us this heritage. They did not focus on the danger, rather the success.

You want danger, talk to the families of Sgt John Harvey, USMC; LCPL George Holmes, Jr., USMC; SSgt Dewey Johnson, USMC. I was on the original roster to take back the US Embassy in Iran. They downsized the roster and took my name off. These are the US Marines that died in my place. They are heroes. The soldiers and Marines in

Iraq are the ones in real danger, not me I believed in my boat and with help from others and God proved it. If you read the whole blog, you will notice we were careful with help not to get in bad weather. Yet we trusted the Intruder. You would too, if you rode one.

My brother Bob never thought we would go all the way to Bermuda, he thought we would turn around at the first big waves. That is what changed his mind, big waves. The Intruder took them flawlessly. We went 1547 miles of open ocean, according to our GPS, and by God's grace never felt in danger at all. We broke NO LAWS AND DISOBEYED NO AUTHORITY. We had more than the required safety equipment. We were in constant communication with the Bermuda equivalent of our coast guard by their request, and they were in constant contact with our Coast Guard, we were tracked all the way back to New York Harbor. I think they were a little surprised that we made it, but both offices told us that we did a great job. The Coast Guard is an absolutely excellent organization. Their Search and Rescue teams save countless lives and risk their own without reservation, and they love doing it. They are heroes. I would never disgrace them. Yes, they and half a dozen more government representatives tried to talk us out of finishing the trip. **That is part of their job.** They said we had already traveled more than any unescorted flats boat that they knew of, and should declare victory. However, that was not the plan. We were determined to finish the course, just like Dream Boats will finish its course. It will become a major competitor in the boating industry.

The Intruder is solid boat. It was designed for the strong who want a flats boat that could take mild stormy seas, and still feel safe. Almost every single person who ever looked at our boat didn't think much of it, just like Bob, until they rode in it. Bob learned to feel safe riding into a storm in the dark with the moon and stars blocked out by clouds 300 miles from the nearest shore and never felt in danger. We really could not see anything, with 4-6 foot seas and pouring down rain. However, we were very cold, man were we cold! Did I tell you it was cold? I am a Florida boy, and I tell you it was cold! We had all kinds of cold weather gear, but it was still cold.

I know it is yet to be determined, but I have been told that we set a new world record, and broke it in a two-week period. That is success. For that success, I thank God and all the other people who helped us like Marin Savov, Pete Rostel, Steve and Sandy Holis, Geoffry, Pete Cardil, and many, many others. Please forgive my spelling. Tomorrow after some rest we will post several pictures and a complete summary.

Anonymous said…
Welcome home! We knew you could do it. Al & Pat
May 13, 2007 6:42 am

Brian said….
Glad you made it, I posted this b log from the beginning of your trip on the Florida sportsman forum… here is a link to the thread…
http://outdoorsbest.zeroforum.com/zerothread? Id=6129223 page=1 May 13, 2007

Brian said….
Well that whole link didn't show.. if you go to www.floridasportsman.com and go to the forums, do a search for "A guy taking a 21' flats boat to Bermuda"….;)
May 13, 2007 10:09 am

Anonymous said…
Ralph, I am glad you and your brother made it, so Bravo! However your comments sound more like a southern preacher then the CEO of a company

who wants to sell boats. Using words like 'sissy' is not the type of language I would expect. Maybe your boat is very seaworthy, then again maybe you just got lucky. People have gone over the side of Niagara Falls in barrels, some lived and some didn't. That does not mean that one barrel was better then the other. A bit of humility would be in order….. I was all for your trip but reading your post made me think of nothing more then a braggart who tempted fate and won, this time. May 13, 2007 1:11 pm

Notombstone said….
Good trip, glad to be home. Yes, we got lucky. But to be honest, we had lots of people checking weather for us. And we waited for the right window. May 13,, 2007 3:47 pm

Anonymous said…
Ralph, I read the comments about Niagara Falls, etc, etc. I spent 4 years at sea and I realize that some luck was involved in your success, however you have proved that you have engineered a seaworthy flats boat. Spoilsports and Monday morning quarterbacks cannot diminish what you have accomplished. Big Al
May 13, 2007 5:44 pm

Anonymous said… Hope it all comes together for you, Ralph. Fred H. May 13, 2007 5:46 pm

Anonymous said….
Good job and seems like you have a very seaworthy boat. Just know that some people will not accept risks as you have. Does not mean they are sissys, just the way some people are. I wish I someday can go ahead and make a trip like that. Wish you the best in selling the boats. May 13. 2007 6:06 pm

From Bermuda said....

Ralph and Bob,

All the big boats are coming out of the Caribbean to Bermuda for safe passage. None of those boaters have the character that you guys demonstrated taking on the ocean with a basic boat and your wits, but all take the challenge of the ocean. Something that cannot be challenged, is that you made it, and not without the virtues of your boat. You proved yourself and the Intruder. Call it luck, or call it skill, but with over 1500 miles of ocean passage, your boat proved itself. Good luck, and keep the wetsuit in Florida as memorabilia. All the best, Geoff May 13, 2007 7:20 pm

Anonymous said....

Yeah, but does it raise fish? Long way to go to get skunked. ☺ LOL! May 14, 2007 6:56 am

Mark said....

Still a pair of Yankee Idiots!! May 14, 2007 7:17 am

Notombstone said....

Thanks Jeff for the use of the wetsuit, it really came in handy. Also, I want to thank you again for all you did for us, while staying at the Dinghy and Sports club. Bob

May 14, 2007 7:46 am

Notombstone said...

While many people comment on what we did was dangerous, what they probably don't realize, was all the help from behind the scene. We had people watching our back, with weather check, plotting the best course, making helpful suggestions, and thing we don't even know about. Remember, we could run right across on a relatively small window, not like the girl Donna Lange, we towed out because her motor would not start. Donna is just about to complete her solo trip around the world in a 27 foot sail boat. While we've been back for a couple of days now, she is still out there sailing and will be for a few more days. www.Donnalange.com May14, 2007 7:52 am

Notombstone said...
Another thing, when I went with Ralph, the first thing I asked him, how does he know that the boat is unsinkable. He started to explain about foam injection in the hull. I am a handyman and know all about injected foam, they use it in building really strong roof, anyway. In order for something to sink, it has to be heavier per volume than water. The foam injection makes that impossible. So the main worry was weather we'd get thrown from the boat (we were tied to it with a short line, so we couldn't go in even if we wanted to without unclipping.) The other worry was weather the motor would die. Relatively new motor, but it could still happen. We had a small kicker to keep us moving slowly until help could arrive, but we had agreed we would not call unless we really were in trouble. As long as we could keep a westward heading, we would be fine. We had plenty of food and water. P.S. The Suzuki 115 ran perfectly. May 14, 2007 8:02 am

Anonymous said....
What was the kicker hp and brand? How fast could it push your boat? May 14, 2007 8:53 am

Anonymous said...
Hey Bob, We want to thank you for going along with Ralph – without you this would not have happened! Many, many thanks. A &P May 14, 2007 11:49

Nototombstone said....
A and P get my e-mail from Ralph, I want to find out what you thought of my book that I believe you might have read.
May 14, 2007 8:00 pm

Notombstone said...
Kicker was 6 hp and pushed the boat about 5 miles per hour with about 310 gallons of gas. Not too bad. I bet we could have muscled about 8 or nine if we had under 100 gallons. May 14, 2007 8:03 pm

Anonymous said...
6 hp! Looks like a Nissan or Tohatsu four stroke kicker. Did you go ahead and went with the 20 inch shaft or the 25?
May 14, 2007 6:27 pm

Notombstone said....
Not sure of the length, it was a kicker that Ralph borrowed. It was all black, and started up with no problem, (that's all I cared about. You'll have to ask Ralph about all the specifics) I just came for the ride and never saw the boat in person until he picked me up in Georgia while I was on a camping trip. I only filled in when Patrick had to cancel for family reasons. Ralph lives on the west coast of Florida while I live near Cocoa Beach on the east coast. I've ridden in none of his other model boats, the 23' on his website. A year or so, we were going to go to the Bahamas in it, but canceled due to a time problem. It would have done well on the Bermuda trip too, but I think Ralph has put that model on hold while he pursues the Intruder line.
May 16, 2007 8:01 am

..........Other comments made by Ralph about the trip..........from his web site......

We changed the oil in Bermuda; usually I let a mechanic do it. I did it myself this time; I did not realize I needed to tell the computer that we changed it. The oil light started flashing about 100 miles from Bermuda, 700 miles from shore. We threw out the sea anchor, turned the boat into the waves, 4-6 ft, and checked the oil. It was fine, so I called my mechanic. While we were waiting to call back we fired up our 6 hp kicker. It pushed us a whopping 5 mph. We made a big joke out of it and agreed that if we needed to take it all the way to shore, we were not calling for help.

Obviously, when I called back the mechanic, we realized there was no problem, he told me how to tell the computer we already changed the oil. Truth of the matter cruising at 5 mph would have made fishing possible and extra 4 day vacation!!! The Suzuki 115 ran like a top. It just purred right along. What an engine!

We had a little cubby hole in front of the console that we slept in some, and also used for phone calls you really had to squeeze into it.

....

The workhorse....our four stroke Suzuki 115.....

Notombstone said...
Ralph used the cubby as an office while the seas were fairly small. Once it got bigger, we had to idle for him to make phone calls, because of the splashing, wind, banging and engine noise. At idle, the engine was so quiet you could hardly hear it. Not to say anything about the sometimes 25 mph wind.
May 21, 2007 2:39 pm

....

These are Friday morning about 180 miles from NY City. It is calm, and we could average about 25 mph at 4000 rpm. These are a bunch of dolphins that are about; to come play in our wake. From the number of pictures I took of the motor, you can tell I was impressed with that Suzuki 115 four stroke.

Notombstone said…
Yes, that Suzuki 115 ran so smooth that whenever we were idling, and talking to anyone while in Bermuda, they were shocked when we either turned the motor off or got ready to drive away. They could hardly believe the motor was running. Can't say enough good things about that motor!
May 21, 2007 2:29 pm

…………

….Here we are with the Statue of Liberty. We did a victory lap at the Statue. We found out you can't do that. Three nice Port Authority Officers showed up in a Police Cruiser and wrote us a $75.00 ticket, about 20 – 30 minutes after we got there. It was nice of them to provide the government documentation of our arrival for the World Record Certification. I believe her name was Officer Teeple, who gave us the welcome home paperwork. In Bermuda people asked us to sign a copy of the newspaper with our pictures on it. In NY Harbor, we got to sign a summons. See how much we are alike.

Notombstone said….
We never noticed that the white buoys, that looked like the no-wake, idle speed zone buoys everywhere else, were in fact restricted zone buoys. We were idling, taking pictures, and then we drove over to the shore across from the Statue of Liberty, looking for the Liberty Park Boat Ramp, no signs visible from the water, except the white no-wake buoys. Looking for

our uncle who was going to pick us up, we drove back through the restricted zone, (buoy missing all together at the corner), where we drove back into restricted zone, later, we found out from the locals, that the sign had been missing for quite some time. We then drove underneath a small bridge and soon were visited by the authorities. In the end, they were really nice, excerpt for the ticket. We learned, in New York Harbor, read your charts. May 21, 2007 2:18pm

Notombstone said....
In the top picture of this series, if you click on the picture, you can see three dolphins or pilot whales playing in the wake. May 21, 2007 2:24 pm

Anonymous said...
Guys... I'm a Bermudian living in NYC... I'll pay that ticket for you! Contact me at michelson77@hotmail.com
May 17, 2007 1:17 pm

Thursday, May 17, 2007
Ultimate Bermuda Challenge Perspective

Many people have a little trouble realizing just how far Bermuda is from North Carolina and back to New York Harbor. We thought the picture might put it in perspective. Bob and I trusted this 21 ft Flats boat (Intruder 21) to get us there and back. In the boating community large areas of shallow water are called "Flats." Boats designed to run in these flats are called "Flats Boats." The Intruder 21 handled the waves perfectly. The pictures below are leaving North Carolina weighted down by almost two thousand pounds of fuel as well as equipment and food stores. As we burned our fuel off the boat got quite a bit lighter and rode much higher.

Dale said….

My Brothers!!! Glad you made it back and back safe. Thank God! Bermuda is a long way out in the ocean! Dale

May 19, 2007 2:26 pm

Notombstone said…

Thanks, just a long boat ride. May 20, 2007 1:31 am

Frank said….

Guys, how fast were you traveling at night? Did you do any trolling along the way? Boredom must have been the hardest part? June 1, 2007 1:07 pm

Ralph said….

To Frank, We did not troll because we were going too fast. We really did not have time to be bored. There was plenty to do. We traded off driving and trying to sleep. At night we drove the same speed as during the day usually between 13 mph and about 25 regardless of the seas. We came on and off plane the whole way. June 1, 2007 2:03 pm

Frank said….

Ralph, seems like the boat performed great. Have you been getting a lot of boat orders?

June 1, 2007 7:52 pm

Chapter 14
Press Release: from the World Record Academy

Saturday, June 2, 2007

Ralph Brown of Spring Hill, Florida and Bob Brown of Merritt Island, Florida have just been informed by the World Record Academy: The World Record Academy has recognized them as being the holders of: The longest unescorted oceanic crossing of a flats boat.

A flats boat by definition is a single engine (Trolling motors don't count), low profile, open fishing boat, that can operate in less than one foot of water. This particular flats boat, the Intruder 21, made by Dream Boats, Inc., can operate in less than six inches of water.

Many smaller boats have made a longer trip, but they always have either a keel, which keeps them from tipping over or helps them right the boat after tipping over; lots of freeboard, the part above the water; a cabin to get out of the weather; a sail so that they don't have to carry their own fuel; or an escort.

The Brown brothers departed from Atlantic Beach, N. C. at 9:15 am, April 30, 2007 arriving in Bermuda at approximately 1:00 p.m. May 2, 2007. They departed Bermuda May 9, 2007, at 9:30 am and arrived in New York Harbor at 3:15 P.m. May 11, 2007 where they received a ticket from Officer Teeple of the US Park Police around Ellis Island, at 3:50 p.m. The brothers accidentally ventured into restricted waters.

More details can be obtained from the World Record Academy's web site:
(http://www.worldrecordsacademy.org/business/longest_unescorted_oceanic_crossing_in_flats_boat_70139.htm)

"Not really a suicide challenge"

The first time I heard the term suicide mixed up with our trip was from reading the paper while in Bermuda after our fist leg of the trip. Sure I used the word suicide in the title of this book because it was the most commonly used word describing our trip from people not actually on the trip. What would be the point of getting killed? Believe me, this was **NOT A SUICIDE TRIP**, we had no intentions of taking any chances. I'm not a skittish person when it comes to boating even though I'm probably not the best choice or the most experience boater suited for this trip. I was available.

Even though I've been called a dare devil at times, I'm really not. There are hundreds of things that I'm too scared to try; this trip was obviously not one of them. I would not run with the bulls, cliff dive in Acapulco, swim without a cage among great whites, stunt ride a motorcycle on the highway, wrestle a real live gator, be a cop and walk down a dark alley after an armed fugitive, and the list could go on and on.

If at anytime Ralph or I thought we were in trouble we would have turned around and headed for shore and called for help. We both had a lot of confidence in the fact that the boat was unsinkable.

Ralph had been planning this trip for a long, long time (eight months to a year) and he had studied the weather for what they refer to as a window to depart North Carolina. **A trip like this takes a lot of planning to do it safely and we would not recommend anyone attempting anything similar**. The coast guard recommends nothing less than a 30 foot and with two engines; unless it is a sailboat with a cabin and keel. The purpose of this trip was to prove that Ralph had enough confidence in his boat design that it would be able to complete a trip of this magnitude.

Time line of my Trip

Thursday, April 26th	Agreed to go with Ralph; left for Georgia camping.
Friday, April 27th	Hiked
Saturday, April 28th	Hiked; met Ralph, started driving to North Carolina
Sunday, April 29th	Arrived in Atlantic Beach, NC; shopped and rigged the boat
Monday, April 30th	Fueled up; Met mayor and city mgt; left At 9:30; Waited for battleship; left Bay At 10:30; lost wireless camcorder Batteries
Tuesday, May 1st	Halfway at 1:00 pm; Lost hand held Camcorder;
Wednesday, May 2nd	Arrived at Bermuda cut at 1:00; Stayed Grotto Bay Hotel
Thursday, May 3rd	Anne and Phillip left; Read 1st Newspaper article; Met with Tim Smith; Boat inspection; Swizzler Inn; Moved Boat to buoy;
Friday, May 4th	Ocean Sails; Wavebreak; read 2nd Newspaper article; 1st autograph; Pulled Boat out; Weather front coming; Met Donna Lange, mayor and locals at the Dinghy and Sports Club; stayed on Lady J

Saturday, May 5th	Minimark get together; Train tour; Shopped;
Sunday, May 6th	Ralph flew to Florida; Stayed in St.George;
Monday, May 7th	Rained; Shopped; Toured island
Tuesday, May 8th	Windy day, ferries closed; fueled boat; Ralph arrived back; worked on boat
Wednesday, May 9th	TV interview; Customs; left towing Donna Lange; boat got swamped; oil light comes on; Black night sky
Thursday, May 10th	Storm clouds; Rained at night; Cold
Friday, May 11th	Glassed off seas; White sided dolphins; New York arrival; Ticket; Uncle David; Left for Florida
Saturday, May 12th	Woke up in Boston Market parking lot; Drove toward Fla.
Sunday, May 13th	Arrived home at 4:30 am
June 2nd	Received World Record from the World Record Academy
July 18th	Guinness Book of World Records™ agreed To start a new category for: Longest Nonstop oceanic voyage in a flats boat
November 5th	Guinness Book of World Records™ awarded us the record (774 miles) St. Georges, Bermuda to New York Harbor (USA), May 9th-11th, 2007.

Thank you!

Jill for allowing me to go and taking care of everything while I was gone.

Ralph for inviting me.

Peter and Debbie Rostel for lending Ralph their boat.

Anne and Phillip in Bermuda

Patrick for helping Ralph prepare the boat

Marino for helping Ralph prepare and to be on call

Paul for being photographer, video man, web master

Investors from Dreamboats Inc.

Brian Greenberg and John Coco Mgt/owner of Benco Insurance

Mike for driving the Mayor out to see us off

Mayor of Atlantic Beach, N.C. seeing us off

Jim and Cheri for diving the car and trailer

Tony Holt and Hernando Today for allowing me to print their article.

Fupper for mentioning Ocean Sails

Ocean Sails: Steve, Suzanne, Rod, Atmaji and Paul for being our Bermuda sponcers ie. Wave break, weather, computers, pictures, etc

Sam Stangeways, Tim Smith and the Royal Gazette for allowing me to print their articles.

Francis for introducing us to Mark and helping pull the boat out of the water

Mark for his work on the Intruder

The guys from Triangle Dive Shop watching the boat, our stuff and advice.

Jeff for helping with charts, advice, wet suit, etc

All the people from the Sports and Dinghy Club especially Peter who let us stay in his boat. Andrew for helping with a place to park the boat. The Mayor for everything she did. Richard and his Dad, Brian, Sean, Charles, Pete, Donna Lang, the Oatelys, Eugene and many many others.

Pat and Patrick from Grotto Bay for telling us about the Sports and Dinghy Club.

Customs for advice and stamping our passports.

Harbour Radio and their gang of inspector who gave us some good advice and kept track of us on our return and some pictures.

Peter Michelson for paying the restricted zone ticket.

Uncle David for taking care of us in New York and pictures.

Friends that critiqued my rough drafts and inspired me to publish it.

World Record Academy for awarding us the record.

The Beachside Resident Publication for help on the cover and pictures.

About Bob Brown
(author and 1st mate)

I am is 49 years old and has been married to Jill for about 21 years. We have two boys Bryan and Jonathan. The family owns two pets, Casey their golden/labrador retriever and Benny their black and white cat.

I has spent much of my youth around the Banana and Indian rivers and surfing in the Atlantic Oceans in Cocoa Beach, Florida. I am still a surfer and has surfed for over 35 years. My favorite board from my quiver at this time is a 9'0" bisect board I made from a 9'4" board that I broke in half a couple of years ago. It's a little slow paddling, but it rides nice and fits in my work van.

I used to scuba dive a fair amount, but have slowed down because lack of partners, it's expensive and I don't own a motor boat anymore. I've been a certified scuba diver since the 80's. I used to take my 21 foot Bayliner Bowrider (don't own it anymore) out 26 miles to the Pelican Grounds off Cape Canaveral, Florida to bottom fish and dive at 100 plus. Once I caught an 11 pound barnacle crusted lobster there. I still owns an 18 foot Hobie sail boat with a broken mast (Ralph helped him break it after going five miles out in the Ocean). I still use the fiberglass Kayak that I built in Cocoa Beach High School in the 70's.

I am still a handyman/house painter and have been self employed for over 26 years.

About Ralph Brown
(captain and owner/designer of Dreamboats Inc.)

Ralph Brown is also a graduate of Cocoa Beach High School, the class of 1976. He is 48 years old and married to Anne. They have been married for about 18 years. They have two boys, Phillip and Heath and a daughter, Brittany.

Ralph has also grown up in Cocoa Beach, where he also surfed and boated. After high school, he joined the Marines, then went to Hyle's Anderson College where he got a masters degree and eventually ended up in Spring Hill, Florida. (near Tampa).

Ralph started his company several years ago, after running aground and damaging the lower unit of an engine. He wanted to make a boat that could run in shallow water, yet feel safe in the bigger seas. The Intruder 21 is the larger size of his second model of boats. Originally called the Dreamcat, but thinking that the Military and Coast Guard might be interested; it was changed to the Intruder.

Ralph builds his boats next to his office in a boat yard in Hudson, Fla. The purpose of this trip was for publicity, prove his boats seaworthiness, and to try to locate investors. "The world record thing was a bonus!"

This trip was sparked after Ralph got tired of people doubting that his boat could take on swells of six foot. "What would happen if you got caught in a squall several miles out in the bay?"

The reason for the trip out to sea rather then along the coast was because the trip had to be news worthy. (A story that might actually get picked up nationally) And without an escort boat, was to show that we had faith in the boat.

Printed in the United States
96658LV00002B/376-444/A

9 781434 349750